IN MEMORY OF

IMOGENE CHAPMAN

GIVEN BY

MR. & MRS. R. C. CORR

&

MR. & MRS. BRYAN CORR

KATHERINE MANSFIELD

A Study of the Short Fiction

Also available in Twayne's Studies in Short Fiction Series

Twayne's Studies in Short Fiction

Gordon Weaver, General Editor
Oklahoma State University

The multifaceted Katherine Mansfield, by Jeffery T. Dalton. Used with permission of the artist.

KATHERINE MANSFIELD

———— *A Study of the Short Fiction* ————

J. F. Kobler
University of North Texas

TWAYNE PUBLISHERS • BOSTON
A Division of G. K. Hall & Co.

Copyright 1990 by G. K. Hall & Co.
All rights reserved.
Published by Twayne Publishers
A Division of G. K. Hall & Co.
70 Lincoln Street, Boston, Massachusetts 02111

Twayne's Studies in Short Fiction Series, no. 14

Copyediting supervised by Barbara Sutton.
Book design and production by Janet Z. Reynolds.
Typeset in 10/12 Caslon by Compset, Inc.

Printed on permanent/durable acid-free paper
and bound in the United States of America.

First published 1990.
10 9 8 7 6 5 4 3 2 1

Library of Congress Cataloging-in-Publication Data

Kobler, J. F. (Jasper Fred), 1928–
    Katherine Mansfield : a study of the short fiction / J.F. Kobler.
        p.   cm.—(Twayne's studies in short fiction ; no. 14)
    ISBN 0-8057-8325-3
    1. Mansfield, Katherine, 1888–1923—Criticism and interpretation.
2. Short story.   I. Title.   II. Series.
PR9639.3.M258Z74   1990
823'.912—dc20   89-71689
                                                        CIP

Contents

Contents

Preface

J. Middleton Murry, husband and editor of Katherine Mansfield, says in his introduction to *The Short Stories of Katherine Mansfield* that every critic who has "tried to define the quality in her work which makes it so inimitable . . . has been compelled to give up the attempt in despair." Defining the "peculiar quality of her work" as "a kind of *purity*," Murry attributes the purity to his belief that Mansfield "looked upon life" through a glass that was "crystal-clear." He claims that Mansfield was as "natural and spontaneous" in her work as she was in life.[1] Such naturalness and spontaneity being most often associated with childlike innocence, Marvin Magalaner in his book-length study of Mansfield (1971) finds that she is able to examine most of her subjects "with the wide-open, uncomplicated gaze of a child," a method that eliminates from Mansfield's work "the likelihood of philosophical consideration, effectively reduces history to the immediate present, and denies the validity of relevant intellectual speculation in the fiction itself."[2]

This book rests on the commonsense assumption that no adult can write as well as Katherine Mansfield wrote and attract such a widespread and continuing adult audience to her short stories without maturing beyond "something childish but very natural," to borrow the words of the title of one of her most intriguing and important short stories, written early in her career (1913) but not published until 1924, almost exactly a year after her death. Granted, Mansfield wrote many stories about childhood, many of them demonstrating the existence of spontaneous, natural, and innocent emotions in children, but these stories are obviously the products of an adult mind that had moved through and beyond those experiences. Even when, as is apparently most often the case, these stories are based on Kathleen Mansfield Beauchamp's personal experiences growing up in New Zealand, they do not demonstrate merely a sentimental yearning to return to such days. Rather, they represent the spirit of a romantic artist at work, one who believes fully in the necessity to retain some of the spirit and imagination of childhood and to continue to live within the natural world in order to sustain that spirit. A mind and a creative imagination that see the value of childhood and of having fewer learned and more natural responses to the facts of life need not be a childish mind; in fact, it cannot be and produce fiction of the quality Mansfield produced.

In Part 1, I try to let the "readings" of the stories alone make the case for Mansfield's being a romantic writer; however, in Part 2, I make direct connections between her ideas and her works and those of the major English romantic poets William Wordsworth and John Keats, connections similar to those Mansfield herself made. Many readers have apparently been confused by Mansfield's ability to let children— in fact, to let all her characters—speak for themselves in their own medium, while at the same time retaining a remarkable imaginative and linguistic distance from them, especially in the face of the over-whelming evidence of how autobiographical a writer she is, as all truly romantic artists must be. Of course, this peculiar ability to be simul-taneously within and without her characters helps give Mansfield's most successful stories that "inimitable" quality about which all read-ers can circle their various critical wagons without ever breaking through to "defeat" totally any individual story, let alone dominate the nature of her work as a whole. All this book can do is what any piece of criticism can do: discuss, analyze, interpret, and evaluate without ever reducing any story to a formulaic phrase. Such is the nature of all our best fiction: It must always just escape encapsulation; otherwise, it would not be our best fiction.

Reared a New Critic but now largely an apostate to that faith, I try to play some of the roles of those later theorists and practitioners lumped under the rubric of Reader Response Theory. Primarily, I try to respond to individual stories as a reader really does—that is, with the expression of immediate reactions to sentences being consumed at any given moment, with tentative readings of phrases that may well change as additional phrases become available. No reader can know as much at any point in the story as he knows at the end of the story; every reader who has been through a story a dozen times ought to know more than the reader who has been through it once. Although this text will undoubtedly be read by some Mansfield scholars who have read each story more than a dozen times and know a great deal more about Mansfield than I know, the book is aimed not at them but at the be-ginning or occasional reader of Mansfield who wants to test a reading of a given story against the reading given here. Most of Mansfield's major stories and those most often anthologized are read closely in Part

1. Occasional references are made to relationships between a story and Mansfield's own life, but it is not at all a function of Part 1 to demonstrate how autobiographical a writer Mansfield is. Readers of this book who want to know more about Mansfield the woman than can be gleaned (in Part 2) from her own words and those of several individuals who knew her personally may wish to read Antony Alpers's 1980 biography, still the best one on Mansfield. Part 3 of this book consists of excerpts from six pieces of criticism of Mansfield's stories and the reprinting of one entire essay on the major and controversial story "Bliss." They demonstrate various approaches to literary texts and present interpretations that differ from those made in this book.

Mansfield has been credited for a long time and by many readers with being instrumental in the movement toward making form in the short story equal in importance to content. The major movement in the short story from Anton Chekhov in Russia to James Joyce in Ireland, through Katherine Mansfield in England and to Ernest Hemingway in the United States, was away from being "great storytellers" and toward being artisans in crafting a short story. Of course, there is a fundamental discrepancy between seeing Mansfield (as Murry and Magalaner do) as being childlike in her storytelling and seeing her as crafting a form. Children are not generally artisans; artisans are not natural and innocent, although their products may at their best give the appearance of being so simple and unsophisticated that they look like child's play. As early as 1936 David Daiches placed Mansfield firmly within this new movement to "make the content so dependent on the form" as to risk failure because the situation (the story) becomes "worth presenting" only because of the way it is presented. If there seems to be no intrinsic merit in the story line, if there seem to be no plot and little action to carry a reader forward, then the writer's success rests totally on her artistic skills. Daiches, speaking of Mansfield's success with this method, put it this way: "There can be no half measures with this method: the critic cannot say, 'A thoroughly well-told story, though a little pointless,' because the point is so bound up with the telling that if it cannot be brought home the telling has no purpose—indeed, no separate existence—at all."[3]

I hope to demonstrate with the following interpretations of thirty of Mansfield's seventy-three completed stories that she regularly not only overcame the risks inherent in the method but helped raise the art of the short story to new heights.

Throughout Parts 1 and 2 of this text, the many uses of ellipses in quotations are all Mansfield's, unless noted otherwise. In Part 3 the ellipses are mine.

The Bibliography is selective and by no means exhausts the criticism and scholarship devoted to Mansfield's stories. The primary principle of selection was that most listed books and essays are likely to be available in most American college and university libraries.

In all my work on this book, I have been assisted greatly by my wife, Sheila Frazier Kobler, who is my severest critic and most dedicated supporter.

J. F. Kobler

University of North Texas

Notes

1. J. Middleton Murry, introduction to *The Short Stories of Katherine Mansfield* (New York: Knopf, 1976), x.

2. Marvin Magalaner, *The Fiction of Katherine Mansfield* (Carbondale: Southern Illinois University Press, 1971), 124.

3. David Daiches, *New Literary Values* (Edinburgh: Oliver & Boyd, 1936), 84.

Acknowledgments

I am grateful for permission to quote from the following works:

Alfred A. Knopf, Inc.: *The Short Stories of Katherine Mansfield*, by Katherine Mansfield. © 1965 by Alfred A. Knopf, Inc.

Cambridge University Press: *The Letters of D. H. Lawrence*, vol. 2, edited by James T. Boulton. © 1981 by Cambridge University Press.

Doubleday: *Figures in the Foreground*, by Frank Swinnerton. © 1964 by Doubleday, a division of Bantam, Doubleday, Dell Publishing Group, Inc.

Indiana University Press: *Katherine Mansfield*, by Kate Fullbrook. © 1986 by Indiana University Press.

Charles Scribner's Sons: *The Sun Also Rises*, by Ernest Hemingway. Copyright 1926 by Charles Scribner's Sons; copyright renewed 1954 by Ernest Hemingway.

Viking Penguin, Inc.: *The Life of Katherine Mansfield*, by Anthony Alpers. © 1980 by Anthony Alpers. All rights reserved. Reprinted by permission of Viking Penguin, a division of Penguin Books USA, Inc. *Dubliners*, by James Joyce. Copyright 1916 by B. W. Huebsch; definitive text © 1967 by the Estate of James Joyce. All rights reserved. Reprinted by permission of Viking Penguin, a division of Penguin Books USA, Inc. *Women in Love*, by D. H. Lawrence. Copyright 1920, 1922 by David Herbert Lawrence. All rights reserved. Reprinted by permission of Viking Penguin, a division of Penguin Books USA, Inc.

Harcourt Brace Jovanovich, Inc.: *The Diary of Virginia Woolf*, vol. 2, 1920–24, edited by Anne Olivier Bell. © 1978 by Quentin Bell and Angelica Garnet. Reprinted by permission of Harcourt Brace Jovanovich, Inc. "The Love Song of J. Alfred Prufrock" and *East Coker*, by T. S. Eliot. Copyright 1930 by T. S. Eliot. Reprinted by permission of Harcourt Brace Jovanovich.

Part 1

THE SHORT FICTION

The First Book of Stories

Katherine Mansfield's first book of short stories grew out of her forced sojourn in Germany, where with many of the Germans depicted in the stories she underwent a cure at the baths, apparently, in her case, for a pregnancy.[1] Most of the thirteen stories of *In a German Pension* are more satirical than Mansfield's later work; certainly, the satire is more direct and biting, a good deal less subtle than in many later stories. Nor do these early stories offer the variety and complexity of narrative modes that were to become almost a trademark of Mansfield's. They are mostly told through a first-person, female narrator who happens to be English or at least of Anglo-Saxon extraction. Some of the "stories" may not even be short stories to those readers who want to make a distinction between "stories," in which a plot develops or something happens to a character to cause change or bring about an insight, and "sketches" of either a person or a scene, in which the whole remains relatively static.

"Germans at Meat," the first entry in the book, may be a case in point, as it portrays a group of residents of the German pension (a boardinghouse), eating and talking their way through a huge meal. The story, or sketch, however, is more than a simple chronological, gustatory trip without any imposed form.

For example, during the first soup course, before Mansfield gets into the heavy eating of the Germans, the narrator is made to feel that she is defending the traditional, large English breakfast, despite the fact that she characterizes herself as one who "drank a cup of coffee while buttoning my blouse in the morning."[2] This initial exchange between one Englishwoman and a number of Germans of both sexes also introduces the broader conflict between the two nations that was building up in 1910 and leading toward world war in 1914.

A few references in these German stories and even fewer scattered through the other stories are the only evidence that Mansfield was aware of political and military matters in her time. Such matters certainly are of little importance to her fiction. The vastly different values that Mansfield placed on national versus human relationships can be seen at the conclusion of "Germans at Meat." The Germans at the table briefly poke fun at the British army and use as specious proof that they do not want to take over England the fact that they have not yet done so. Having depicted Germans who pick their teeth with hairpins, clean their ears with napkins, and discuss bodily functions with gusto, Mansfield's narrator understandably proclaims that England certainly does "not want Germany" (*KM*, 40) either. The Germans, however, quickly return to their real interests as the "cherry cake with whipped cream" (*KM*, 40) is served, asking the Englishwoman what is her husband's favorite meat. Although she says she has been married three years—which fact carefully distinguishes the narrator from Mansfield, who at the time of her arrival in Bad Worishofen in June 1909 had been married to George Bowden for almost exactly three months (Alpers, 85)—the narrator admits that she does not know what her husband's favorite meat is, because she has never asked him and because "he is not at all particular about his food" (*KM*, 40). The Germans, of course, are shocked and wonder how such an ignorant, uncaring woman can ever expect to keep a husband.

This refrain about the grossness of Germans runs consistently through these first stories. "The Baron" depicts a baron who always eats his meals alone in order to eat more: "I order double portions, and eat them in peace" (*KM*, 44). Asked what he does all day between meals, he replies that he ingests "nourishment in my room" (*KM*, 44).

Mansfield, however, does not simply display grossness for its own sake, even if at times in these stories the satire borders on caricature. In "The Modern Soul" she infuses an eating scene with sexual symbolism, depicting a German professor who gorges himself on both cherries and their inevitable worms, apparently with equal delight. He claims that being a professor allows him to understand the female psychology lying behind the narrator's declining to eat the cherries: "It is your innate feminine delicacy in preferring etherealised sensations. . . . Or perhaps you do not care to eat the worms" (*KM*, 63). The sexually connotative values of cherries and worms are reinforced in the passage when Mansfield has the professor stick the "cherry bag between his knees" and address his companion in the following suggestive way: "If one wishes to satisfy the desires of nature one must be strong enough to ignore the facts of nature. . . . The conversation is not out of your depth? I have so seldom the time or opportunity to open my heart to a woman that I am apt to forget" (*KM*, 63). The lady's English restraint in contrast to the German's excess is successfully captured in Mansfield's phrasing: "I looked at him brightly" (*KM*, 63) and, later, "I was grateful, without showing undue excitement" (*KM*, 64). Fortunately, the Englishwoman is saved from further advances by the appearance on the scene of Sonia, the modern soul of the title.

In this very early story Mansfield demonstrates her lifelong distrust of too much modernity in women, including its obvious presence in her own life. The narrator in these German stories seems to be circumspect, trained in the better social graces, and traditional in her sexual reticence. In contrast, Sonia Godowska is a "furiously sapphic" (*KM*, 69) woman who declares herself in love with her own tragedy (her mother), cursed by her own genius, and doomed by that genius to marry only "a man who would be for me a pillow—for genius cannot hope to mate" (70). This story may be the first fictional examination that Mansfield made of at least two sides of her own multifaceted personality, but it is not the last. The merest suggestion of lesbianism in the story also relates to some of the writer's experiences of girlhood (Alpers, 46–47).

In many ways, Mansfield must have seen herself as both the traditional narrator and the modern woman. Especially at this early time in her life (she was twenty-two), she demonstrates her fear that her artistic talent is no more genuine than Sonia's self-proclaimed genius. In poking fun at Sonia, Mansfield may be telling herself that the very story in which she is doing so is not much better than Sonia's musical performance. As the next decade of writing would reveal, Mansfield had a genius that in 1910 had not yet ripened but whose potential she so strongly felt that she could simultaneously poke fun at (a) the traditional wife and woman that her mother represented and that she knew she did not want to be and (b) the artist that she was afraid she was only pretending to be and might never really become. Discussions of later stories will show how Mansfield's questioning her own roles continued to be a part of her fiction.

If the pretentious modern woman is a frequent inhabitant of Mansfield's stories, so also is the naive young woman—a character often not much more than a child. The naïf makes an early appearance in the story "At Lehmann's." Young enough to have natural pink coloring in her cheeks, Sabina is maid and waitress for both the home and the café of the Lehmanns. As she waits on tables, she moves "with that magical child air about her, that delightful sense of perpetually attending a party" (*KM*, 73). Frau Lehmann is about to have another baby. Sabina knows that women do not have babies without having husbands, "but what had the man got to do with it?" (*KM*, 74). Thus Mansfield portrays a complete innocent. When a young man comes to the café and pays attention to Sabina, she is, despite her total lack of understanding about sex, emotionally and physically moved by his presence: "His restless gaze wandering over her face and figure gave her a curious thrill deep in her body, half pleasure, half pain. . . . She wanted to stand there, close beside him, while he drank his wine" (*KM*, 74). Thus Mansfield also depicts natural, physical yearnings in young women, those very yearnings that her parents' generation would have warned her to avoid at all costs and that much of her own generation was telling her to obey at absolutely no cost—or, if the voices were sufficiently Freudian, to obey lest there be great cost.

"At Lehmann's" is certainly no sketch; it has a distinct plot involving what will happen to Sabina's virginity and a paralleling and contrasting structure in the impending birth of a baby to the very fat Frau Lehmann. The contrast between the attention that the young man is paying to Sabina and the lack of attention that Herr Lehmann is paying to his wife may be a little obviously displayed. Frau Lehmann is every woman in the conventional and traditional wisdom of that time, accepting her fate as "nothing" beside her husband, who is playing cards at Snipold's. She says, "Dear heaven, leave him alone. I'm nothing. I don't matter" (*KM*, 76). Being with Sabina, in contrast, matters very much to the young man, who remains nameless, not only to show the universality of his pursuit but also to imply that even if she succumbs to his blandishments, Sabina will never bear his name. Realistically, too, such a young man would not reveal his name.

Mansfield continues to contrast the young man's labors to seduce Sabina and Frau Lehmann's to produce her child. In fact, the birth of the baby may save Sabina from the young man's most persistent effort to seduce her, but Mansfield leaves the case open, not even implying that Sabina would have lost her struggle had it not been interrupted by "a frightful, tearing shriek" (*KM*, 78) from the room above. As the young man attempts to have his way with Sabina in the ladies' cloakroom, she is described at various points by Mansfield as "breathing like a frightened little animal," as thrilling to a "strange tremor" (*KM*, 78), as wanting to burst out crying or go on laughing—as, in short, suffering and enjoying what are apparently the very mixed and common feelings of many young women in such circumstances. Just before the shriek from Frau Lehmann sends Sabina shrieking from the room, the young man has placed his hands on her breasts and the room seems "to swim around Sabina" (*KM*, 78).

Mansfield leaves the thwarted seduction open to wide interpretation, including the possibility that Sabina might have enjoyed the actual intercourse, had it taken place. The contrast, however, between the attentions of the young man to a pretty girl and the lack of attention paid by a husband to a fat wife says very strongly that whatever pleasures might come to young ladies in closets ought to be balanced against what happens to old wives in childbirth. During the course of the story Sabina thinks how "very sweet" it might be "to have a little baby to dress and jump up and down" (*KM*, 74). But just before she has this thought, she hears Frau Lehmann's heavy footsteps above her and worries that "she herself should one day look like that—feel like that!" (*KM*, 74). Thus, in one of her earliest stories Mansfield poses eternal questions about love, sex, and marriage that simultaneously have no answers and all the answers in the world. Mansfield's own strange marriage just months earlier; her pregnancy, undoubtedly caused by a man other than her husband; and the loss of her baby to miscarriage or stillbirth in Germany (Alpers, 98)—all must have entered into the writing of what may be the best story in this early collection.

Some of the same male chauvinism toward the beaten-down wife and her concerns about pregnancy exist in "Frau Brechenmacher Attends a Wedding." In one wonderfully sarcastic sentence Mansfield captures the male-female relationship that she must have seen so often and, as a later discussion will demonstrate, not just in Germany: "Herr Brechenmacher, completely overawed by this grand manner [at the wedding], so far forgot his rights as a husband as to beg his wife's pardon for jostling her against the banisters in his efforts to get ahead of everybody else" (*KM*, 58).

The wedding of Theresa, who brings one child with her to the ceremony and is implicitly pregnant again, makes Frau Brechenmacher remember her own wedding and her emotions at that time. Theresa, by the way, is believed to be pregnant by one man but marrying another, a situation about which Frau Brechenmacher says, "That's not how a wedding should be; it's not religion to love two men" (*KM*, 60). Remembering how she and her husband "had come home together" their first night of marriage, Frau Brechenmacher mutters a question to herself, "What is it all for?" (*KM*, 61). Mansfield shows how important the question really ought to be to this woman, while also indicating how at that time and in that place Frau Brechenmacher understands the pointlessness of raising such questions: "Not until she had reached home, and prepared a little supper of meat and bread for her man did she stop asking herself that silly question" (*KM*, 61). The story concludes with another strong indictment of how a very young Mansfield must have already experienced men treating women during the sexual act: "Then even the memory of the wedding faded quite. She lay down on the bed and put her arm across her face like a child who expected to be hurt as Herr Brechenmacher lurched in" (*KM*, 62).

Of the concluding five stories of *In a German Pension*, only one, "The Advanced Lady," is set within the pension and has a truly German atmosphere. The other four are "German" only in the names of the characters, as if Mansfield had run out of material from her time in Bavaria but needed more German stories to fill out the book to respectable size and to maintain thematic unity. One of the stories, in fact, is recognized generally by critics as being Mansfield's first fictional journey back to New Zealand.

"A Birthday" may indeed be Mansfield's somewhat bitter look at her own arrival in the world, although the baby born in the story is a boy. If the story represents a movement backward in time for subject matter, it also demonstrates a movement forward in form that perhaps began taking place from late 1910 to early 1911, when Mansfield was twenty-two to twenty-three years of age. Of the seven truly German stories, first published in *New Age* between 3 March and 18 August 1910 and included in this volume, five are told by a first-person narrator and two omnisciently, although at times approaching a kind of interior monologue close to what Mansfield would later employ as her primary mode of narration. "The Modern Soul" and "The Advanced Lady," both satirical of modern, liberated, but terribly precious women, are also German stories written in the first person, although they may have been written a little later than the others. "The Modern Soul" was first printed in *New Age* on 22 June 1911, and "The Advanced Lady" was not published prior to its appearance in book form. Mansfield's *Journal* and her *Scrapbook* are of no assistance in determining when these stories were composed, because she destroyed most of those personal materials for the period between 1909, when she returned to England from New Zealand, and 1914. Nor do the published letters provide information about the times of composition. It may be conjectured that since "The Swing of the Pendulum" and "A Blaze" were not published prior to the release of *In a German Pension* in December 1911, they were composed too late in that year to receive periodical publication.

Whenever composed, the latter two stories portray in two distinct narrative forms similarly confused young women. Love has them in torment. The interior monologue of "The Swing of the Pendulum" is probably Mansfield's first extended and successful use of that narrative point of view. "A Blaze" is written almost as if it were a one-act play, containing almost nothing but dialogue and short narrative passages that read largely like stage directions. Both stories demonstrate how seriously Mansfield was working to shape her stories through form.

That the interior monologue worked better for Mansfield than the objective telling did is proved by her adopting the former for the bulk of her later stories. Both "The Swing of the Pendulum" and "A Blaze," however, show that Mansfield was well settled into beginning in medias res without introducing or describing characters and without relying on any semblance of the "once upon a time" formula. These two stories begin with the sentences "The landlady knocked at the door" (*KM*, 109) and "Max, you silly devil, you'll break your neck if you go careering down the slide that way" (*KM*, 119). Viola in "The Swing of the Pendulum" is despondently in her room at ten "in the morning of a grey day" (*KM*, 110), being hounded by her landlady for the rent and enraged by a "condescending" letter from Casimir, apparently her lover. She is interrupted by a knock at the door while washing her face and experimenting with a nonserious suicide method of "drowning in a bucket." A man with an "infectious" smile is asking for some other woman, who does not live there. Dripping wet with "her petticoat bodice unbuttoned" (*KM*, 111), Viola baffles herself by asking the man to wait at the door while she dries off a little. After some self-conscious dialogue between them, she does shut the door, to start thinking about the sickness of herself and Casimir and of their relationship, in contrast with what she wildly imagines to be this "amazingly happy," "jolly" "sane and solid" (*KM*, 112) man at her door. Although the reader may be inclined to take Viola's thoughts about herself and Casimir at face value—that is, as honest evaluations of the way things really are between them—Viola's sudden high estimation of a stranger at the door ought to serve as a cautionary flag. Her inability to understand her own feelings and be honest with herself, together with her own awareness of her shortcomings and powerlessness to do anything about them, is captured in these three sentences: "I wish I could step outside the whole affair and just judge it—then I'd find a way out. I certainly was in love with Casimir. . . . Oh, be sincere for once" (*KM*, 112).

Perhaps the main point of the story is that Viola has no more will than a pendulum, that she is driven by some mechanism outside her control, of which she is but the visible agent. Certainly her argument with herself about what she really wants and needs and what she really feels and believes makes no forward movement toward a resolution. She swings back and forth, but "the figure of the strange man rose before her—would not be dismissed" (*KM*, 113). During some three pages of interior monologue, Mansfield does a remarkable job of handling a very new technique; however, she does slip at least once in this early story, when she allows her narration to leave Viola's consciousness to provide this sentence: "And instead of the ordinary man who had spoken with her at the door her mind created a brilliant, laughing image, who would treat her like a queen" (*KM*, 114). Surely every reader by this point knows that Viola is desperately creating something good out of something that is at best unknown. Surely many readers by now suspect that the man is somehow going to demonstrate to Viola before the story is over that he is not what she so desperately imagines him to be, a lover who can save her from herself and who looks "as though he could order a magnificent dinner" (*KM*, 114). The absurdity of what Viola thinks about this stranger renders almost silly what she has experienced so far.

Sensing that the man may still be outside her door, she puts on "a long white gown" and opens the door, not knowing "what was going to happen" but thinking what fun it can be as she and this stranger play "a delicious game" (*KM*, 114). Of course, he is still there, and after some discussion of getting wood for the fire from the landlady, they enter Viola's room, which, in her eyes only, is "quite changed." Everything looks so different that Viola remembers "childish parties when they had played charades" (*KM*, 115), thus continuing the idea of games and probably demonstrating how childish Viola really can be. The man invites her to go driving the next day, to which she agrees because "after all—this was just a game" (*KM*, 116). The game changes, or Viola starts to lose, or maybe it stops being a game and becomes "life" when she refuses an invitation to sit on his knee. Things rapidly deteriorate when he offers her two hundred marks for a kiss, and she demands that he leave. Instead, he physically attacks her, holding her against the wall and pressing "upon her with all the weight of his body" (*KM*, 118). The game seems likely to become a rape, until she bites his hand.

What might be called the chaotic characterization of Viola continues as the story concludes back in her mind. She is flooded by "a sensation of glorious, intoxicating happiness," which might seem to many readers an abnormal substitute for fear and panic, as she threatens to bite him again, if he will not leave. Once he is gone, she laughs and dances "about the room" (*KM*, 118). She wishes that Casimir "could have seen us" and realizes that her "feeling of rage and disgust against Casimir" is gone. Again she goes into her imagination, thinking of three o'clock when Casimir will arrive and she can run to him, exclaiming, "My blessed one! Of course we are bound to win. Do you love me still? Oh, I have been horrible lately" (*KM*, 119).

How can any reader believe at this point that Viola's real response to Casimir's arrival will resemble this imagining? By the time he arrives, she will surely have gone through many more mind games with herself, coming up with any number of possible plays. The story does, indeed, present a tortured and confused mind in the person of Viola, but it lacks the subtlety of narration that is found in later Mansfield stories. After all, Viola has almost been raped, but Mansfield seems to be saying that she would have brought it on herself. It is difficult today to believe that Mansfield wanted this story to say what it probably does to many readers: The man is not really at fault. Viola does not take at all seriously what might have happened to her; it surprises me that Mansfield seems to have taken it no more seriously.

Rape seems not to have been on Mansfield's mind when she wrote the story, but many of her own emotional confusions and torments may have been at work during 1909 to 1910, when she was in various ways in love with at least four men other than her husband. Although the evidence is not entirely clear, Mansfield was probably physically intimate with Floryan Sobieniowski, Garnet Trowell, and Francis Heinemann; her relationship with William Orton appears to have been more platonic (Alpers, 92, 101, 117, 119). Whether Mansfield meant to portray her own confusion about love in Viola is less important than the fact that the author certainly seems to have understood that portion of Viola's problem from firsthand experiences. Although the temptation to see nothing but bathos in Viola's confusion or even to label her as crazy may be strong in many readers, it should perhaps be resisted for Mansfield's sake.

"A Blaze" is a much more obvious and unsatisfying story, one that primarily concerns the visit, one day, of Max with Elsa, the wife of Victor. Max is undoubtedly sincere in his intent to seduce Elsa, an end he accuses her of leading him toward: "You've tormented me—you've led me on—offering me everything and nothing at all" (*KM*, 122). The more insistent Max becomes, the more reticent Elsa is, telling him, for example, that he has "no right to talk" to "another man's wife" (*KM*, 122) that way. Like Viola, Elsa successfully resists being overcome physically, but shortly after she has repulsed Max she utters the most interesting words in the story, because of the way they can tantalize a reader into wanting to know how closely Elsa's self-description can be applied to Mansfield's emotions about herself at this time in her life:

> I'll make a confession. Every word you have said [about her leading him on] is true. I can't help it. I can't help seeking admiration any more than a cat can help going to people to be stroked. It's my nature. I'm born out of my time. And yet, you know, I'm not a *common* woman. I like men to adore me—to flatter me—even to make love to me—but I would never give myself to any man. I would never let a man kiss me . . . even. (*KM*, 123)

One final story from *In a German Pension* needs mention because of the large amount of critical attention it has received.[3] "The Child-Who-Was-Tired" certainly owes something to the great Russian short story writer Anton Chekhov, but what exactly it owes has been much debated and will not be argued again here. Left to its own merits, the story—about how a crying baby is smothered by its very young nurse— would cause much less excitement, not being one of Mansfield's strongest efforts.

Nor, of course, does this whole first book of stories represent Mansfield at her best, as she herself stated in February 1920 in a letter to Murry about not wanting the book reissued because it is "immature," "positively juvenile, and besides that it's not what I mean; its a lie." In her next letter she acquiesced to Murry's apparent pleading but said she would need to write an introduction to point out that it was an "early, early work."[4]

In a German Pension was not, in fact, reprinted before Mansfield's death in January 1923. That she saw these stories as merely foreshadowing her later ones, perhaps even as being immature, is easily understood. Less easily grasped are the reasons that she considered the book "a lie" and not what she meant to say. On the surface her evaluation sounds more concerned with content than with form, which was certainly in a developmental stage at that time. Can form ever be called "a lie"? Since Mansfield's forte and significance in short story writing appear to lie largely in her own peculiar blending of form and content, the possible meanings of her assertion about a book being a lie are not easily determined. In fact, it may well be best to investigate in subsequent sections some of the kinds of truths that Mansfield talks about wanting to achieve and that she indeed may have achieved in her later stories, before trying to discover what kind of lie she saw herself telling in a collection of the early ones.

The New Zealand Stories

With one exception, the dozen stories that Katherine Mansfield wrote between 1911, when *In a German Pension* was published, and March 1915, when she began "The Aloe" in Paris, were not collected in book form until 1924, when Murry printed *Something Childish and Other Stories*, a year after Mansfield's death. The one exception is "The Little Governess," which Mansfield selected for inclusion in *"Bliss" and Other Stories* (1920). Mostly minor stories, looked at collectively today they show Mansfield searching for her métier. "Pension Seguin" and "Bains Turcs" ("Turkish Baths") look back in tone and content to her Bavarian experiences, and "The Woman at the Store" and "Ole Underwood" look even further back to New Zealand. These latter two are stories of a strong naturalistic bent, revealing none of the satire of the German stories.

Mansfield described what happened on 24 March 1915 as the Muses descending upon her, causing her to fall "into the open arms of my first novel," "The Aloe."[5] The circumstances of her life may also have had something to do with her having "a great day" of writing.[6] Her short affair with Francis Carco, a dedicated Bohemian writer and also a friend of Murry's, was over; her relationship with Murry had improved; and although her physical health was still poor, she had moved back to Paris alone with firm intentions of writing (Alpers, 177–79). Surely the greatest influence, however, on this sudden flowing of creative juices was the presence in England of her twenty-one-year-old brother, Leslie Beauchamp, who had arrived in February for military training, opening the doors of memory to their childhoods in New Zealand. If Chummie's coming back into Mansfield's life was instrumental in her beginning to produce some fifty pages of manuscript in Paris, his death in a hand-grenade accident in France on 7 October 1915 effectively ended her work until she could recover from the shocking loss (Alpers, 182–83). The significance of Chummie, his death, and Mansfield's recognition of what she had to do with her material is caught in this passage from her *Journal*: "But all must be told with a sense of mystery, a radiance, an afterglow because you, my little sun of it, are set. You have dropped over the dazzling brim of the world. Now I must play my part."[7] The playing of her part in turning the manuscript of "The Aloe" into the published *Prelude* began in February 1916 and took until 10 July 1918, the day Virginia and Leonard Woolf sent out the first copies of the hand-set book.

Although Mansfield knew, as she said in a letter to the Honorable Dorothy Brett, artist and close friend, that she had something here "more or less my own invention," her statement about this new form says more about what she "tried to catch" from her people and her homeland than how she actually caught it (O'Sullivan, 1:331). Mansfield's feeling of inadequacy in describing exactly how her prose works in *Prelude* and later stories has been duplicated down through the years by most critics, who see very well the word-magic occurring in front of their eyes but can catch in their own words only glimmerings of how that magic works. Most obviously and simply it involves the removal of a narrator as an active and direct agent in the telling of the story. The narrator, whether Katherine Mansfield or an alter ego of the author, is present in most of the stories written from the German experiences, clearly visible and audible in the first-person pronoun. The events in these stories do not just happen; they are shaped by the narrator's view of how they happened.

Of course, in reality Mansfield's consciousness cannot possibly be missing from *Prelude* or any other story. Some human consciousness has to be at work in all stories, unless we are going to move beyond magic and start fantasizing about muses and stories that write themselves. The magic lies in Mansfield's being able to move prose fiction closer to the dramatic form, in which characters can speak for themselves. One of the enduring fictions of the theater was transformed before our very eyes by Mansfield and many other twentieth-century writers into a now-enduring technique of literature.

Despite these general "truths" about the new prose fiction, there is still the magical truth that the "nonvoice" of Katherine Mansfield in her stories has a different sound from that of other authors—say, James Joyce, to name one of her near-contemporaries. The reader of well-tuned ear and even a modicum of experience will never confuse the sounds of a Joyce and a Mansfield story. Murry's notion, quoted earlier, that Mansfield was able to write as she did because she looked at life through a "crystal-clear" set of lenses is just not possible. Neither could she have retained a child's vision despite her adult experiences; whatever her stories may lack in tedious, cold, philosophical positions, they are not expressions of a child's mind. If Mansfield lacks a dogmatic view of life and, with Laura in "The Garden Party," finds the meaning of life inexpressible in a mere phrase, so much the better. If Mansfield did not blindly accept the old-fashioned idea of a central self that needed discovering but did lean toward belief in the possibility of multiple selves, so much the better—at least for a fiction that tries to let every character present herself or himself directly through word and action but without turning those characters loose on the stage.

Prelude begins, "There was not an inch of room for Lottie and Kezia in the buggy" (*KM*, 219). This is no storyteller's opening line but a magician's interception of a reader's eye in midpassage.

Compare that Mansfield sentence with the opening sentences of the first two stories in Joyce's *Dubliners:* "There was no hope for him this time: it was the third stroke" ("The Sisters") and "It was Joe Dillon who introduced the Wild West to us" ("An Encounter").[8] Although each sentence begins in the middle of an action, describing the action without any comment on it, the reader soon discovers in "The Sisters" and the line from "An Encounter" makes explicit that the Joyce stories both have first-person narrators. Mansfield's does not. So who in the story knows there is "not an inch of room" for what most readers will surely assume to be two children? Every character involved in the action can see the lack of room, but the reader does not yet know who those persons are.

Only as the paragraph develops does the reader learn who is taking part in the scene. The reader who thinks of this as a staged scene happening before his very eyes can better grasp how the magic works. The characters on the stage would be discovering the lack of room by looking at the buggy, simultaneously with the audience's learning the same thing through the same act of looking. In effect, the characters in the story are learning things about their scene at the same moment the reader is; there is no privileged viewpoint of some omniscient narrator, telling about events that have already occurred. The action has not previously taken place; it is taking place.

Not everyone involved in this simple action, however, knows the same things for the same reasons. For example, the statement that "Linda Burnell could not possibly have held a lump of a child on [her lap] for any distance" is loaded with precise implications and with an exposure of Linda's mental processes that a theater audience could not possibly "know" from what it physically sees. But a theater audience would know something that the reading audience can only assume:

that Linda Burnell is pregnant. Physically, then, it would be dangerous for her to try to hold any child on her lap for very long. Are these her children? A theater audience might know from the list of characters in the playbill; from the scene itself and from the relative ages of the two adult females, our hypothetical theater audience might guess that the two little girls (the reading audience must assume their femaleness from their names) are the children of the pregnant woman. A character named Pat appears. The name may be either male or female, but maleness is assumed by the reader because Pat is physically strong enough to swing two persons up "on top of the luggage." But what about that phrase *a lump of a child* in the sentence quoted above? To whom are these darling little girls (the theater audience can see them; the reading audience assumes they are darlings from this paragraph and verifies it in the next one) mere "lumps"? To their mother, Linda, of course, as the story will continue to demonstrate but which fact may be assumed here at the beginning. Linda implies that the girls cannot make this trip because the "bags and boxes" on the floor of the carriage "are absolute necessities that I will not let out of my sight for one instant"— meaning that having Lottie and Kezia out of sight may also be happily out of mind, for Linda.

This extended analysis of one paragraph is meant to demonstrate several things about Mansfield's prose in *Prelude* and many subsequent stories: It is finely crafted; the reader must be constantly alert as to what the text is doing to perception; the point of view is multiple and shifting; and the nonexistent narrator must be watched closely, lest she sneak in and do a little sleight of hand. If the form of the story is complex and tantalizing, it only fits with the content and with the author's ambivalence toward her homeland and her own family members, who without a doubt are represented by the Burnells of the story.

Mansfield's mother's name was Annie Burnell Dyer Beauchamp. The story itself is entitled *Prelude* because the life depicted here for Kezia (Katherine) and the members of her family is but the prelude to later life and fiction. In the story Mansfield not only begins to develop her new style but creates events that will be instrumental in the development of her thematic interests in later stories. One of those themes involves the apparently inherent difficulties with love between men and women, a theme analyzed in detail later in Part 1, as it occurs in several stories. In *Prelude* Linda and Stanley Burnell convincingly represent the masculine and feminine principles that Mansfield so often depicts in her stories. Despite the absence of any direct authorial judgment in the story, every reader knows that Stanley Burnell is depicted unfavorably as he goes about being the kind of man his New Zealand (and English and American) society of the late nineteenth century expected him to be. He does nothing around the house except carve the duck at dinner, because women "never seemed to care what the meat looked like afterwards" (*KM*, 254). He demands that his mother-in-law get him his slippers. He is implicitly compared by his wife to her dog, of whom she is very fond, but she wishes the dog "wouldn't jump at her so, and bark so loudly and watch her with such eager, loving eyes" (*KM*, 258). Stanley hates servility in men but requires it of his women. In short, he is portrayed as the typical and societally admired male chauvinist of the time. No matter how typical he may be, the power of his portrait and the fundamental fact that he paints his own picture keep the typical from shading into the stereotypical. Mansfield's method causes Stanley to condemn himself through word and deed, while at the same time Linda's attitude toward him (again without externally imposed narrative directives) softens his chauvinistic personality.

What Linda does to and for her own portrait while helping to color Stanley's is more complex and probably more interesting to most readers than anything Stanley does. Although Mansfield guides her story into Stanley's mind on occasion, it is clear from both the quantity and the quality of Linda's inner life that Mansfield takes Linda's interior world far more seriously than she takes Stanley's. While it is true that his great and surely superficial happiness in his present life stands in contrast to Linda's deep unhappiness, that simple distinction is not the only dividing factor that Mansfield crafts between the two.

Any analysis of what Mansfield's skillful maneuvering of Linda's and Stanley's outer words and actions means in relation to their inner lives is made additionally tricky by the problem of determining causes and effects. Narrators often do such work for the reader (as Mansfield's surrogate does in many of the *German Pension* stories), but here there is no guiding voice. When the Burnells wake up to a beautiful morning after their first night in their new house, Stanley is "enormously pleased" and his obviously superficial, smug thought process goes like this: "Weather like this set a final seal on his bargain. He felt, somehow, that he had bought the lovely day, too—got it chucked in dirt cheap with the house and ground" (*KM*, 232). Mansfield and the reader both know that Stanley has his rational causes and effects badly confused, as undoubtedly Stanley would also know if he stopped to things in another way. Although he thinks an obviously silly thing here, it can speak well for his personality in a reader's mind, because his natural feeling stands in violent conflict with his pursuit of the practical. In a later incident, the effect that societal training has on Stanley in causing him to do something contrary to a natural and, by implication, good impulse is demonstrated when he thinks "he wouldn't mind giving" his driver Pat "a handful" of cherries but counters this feeling with the safe rationalization that he had better wait until Pat "had been with him a bit longer" (*KM*, 241–42). In Stanley's defense and in further explanation of Mansfield's success as creator of him, it should be recognized that Stanley is too happy in his actual living at this point to worry (or think) much about the nature of life. Does he not demonstrate life daily in the very doing of it? Why ruminate when one can dominate?

Almost naturally, it seems, Linda and her sister Beryl Fairfield do a great deal of thinking, mostly about how unhappy they are in their present conditions. Yet Mansfield depicts their two minds as being quite different. Linda is clearly the more sympathetic of the two, perhaps largely because she is more honest with herself but also because Mansfield plays on the female-male situation to show that Linda is unhappy in a condition (marriage) that Beryl yearns for. Nothing in the characterization of the sisters even implies they are so different that Beryl would be happy if they changed places. Rather, Beryl is established as the romantic unmarried woman who believes marriage cannot help but bring happiness, even though she lives daily with evidence to the contrary. Beryl seems to blame Linda for Linda's unhappiness, but overall the story shows that Mansfield blames the kind of marriage that most women like these had to make as being the cause of Linda's current unhappiness and implicitly predicts that in marriage Beryl would encounter the same life and thoughts. Although some readers think badly of Linda because she does not love her children, surely in so casting her, Mansfield becomes an early questioner of another assumption of that society: that all women have a maternal instinct.

Linda's marriage has produced those emotions in her and her honesty about them; the absence of such feelings in Beryl and the presence in her of romantic notions about how marriage, as such, will bring her happiness contribute to the reader's feeling that this kind of marriage is the culprit, not either of the partners personally. The fault lies, the story says, not with the women and not with this husband but with all traditional marriages between unequal partners. Almost no other kind occurs in Mansfield's stories; their success rate is exceedingly low. Although Mansfield regularly goes into Linda's mind, the following quotation well demonstrates the nature of Linda's feelings and Mansfield's portrayal of them as completely honest and natural. The passage follows Linda's recognition that despite "all her love and respect and admiration" for Stanley, she hates him; the action that brings all these thoughts to the surface is his responding with far too much joy and enthusiasm to her simple request that he light a candle: "It had never been so plain to her as it was at this moment. There were all her feelings for him, sharp and defined, one as true as the other. And there was this other, this hatred, just as real as the rest. She could have done her feelings up in little packets and given them to Stanley. She longed to hand him that last one, for a surprise. She could see his eyes as he opened that" (*KM*, 258).

Linda will not and cannot tell Stanley she hates him. As she recognizes with silent laughter, life (the life that their society forced on such women) is absurd. This kind of life is, indeed, absurd for a woman. Too many women in too many Mansfield stories suffer these indignities for Linda to be seen as strange and unusual, as a misfit in this world.

Linda's unmarried sister Beryl yearns after exactly this sort of life. The great irony is that she already has it, but the man who works to supply her food and shelter is not her own man. Things would be different if Beryl had a husband of her own, she thinks; but the story says that they would not be. Mansfield establishes through the thoughts of these two sisters a basic difference in attitudes. Linda, suffering to learn it but learning it just the same, knows that she is a complex being who can both love and hate her husband; she knows, as the passage quoted above demonstrates, that she has no true self to be discovered. Beryl has not yet learned that the concept of a true self is a Platonistic ideal that has no bearing on real human beings. She thinks of herself as "always acting a part." She tells herself that she is not ever her real self. She upbraids herself for putting on a show "for Stanley's benefit" just the previous evening; "when he was reading the paper her false self had stood beside him and leaned against his shoulder on purpose" (*KM*, 262).

In this societal structure, the current "rules" about marriage mean that despite her misery Linda will "go on having children and Stanley will go on making money and the children and the gardens will grow bigger and bigger"; likewise, Beryl will go on believing that her real self does not want to steal her sister's husband, that only her false self would dare to "put her hand over his, pointing out something so that he should see how white her hand was beside his brown one" (*KM*, 262). The Beryl that she believes she really is and has achieved at "tiny moments" is "rich and mysterious and good" (*KM*, 262), and life is also all of those things.

Life for the mother of these two women—the grandmother of Kezia—is, in contrast, wanting her pantry shelves well supplied with her homemade jam. Totally practical and the hardest-working member of the family, Mrs. Fairfield immediately tackles the kitchen of the new house and soon everything in the kitchen has been arranged in patterns. She surveys her work, smiles, and thinks how satisfactory it is.

Why is Mrs. Fairfield so calm, self-contained, practical, and hard-working? Since this story goes no more often into her consciousness than it does into Stanley's, a superficial reading might be that Mansfield no more knew what makes stoical grandmothers tick than she knew what makes men like Stanley tick. Realizing the possible danger to her credibility of employing this method of writing to go into the minds of characters she could not "know" internally, Mansfield simply avoided trying to do so. Such an interpretation has to be tempting to any reader who is trying to avoid the issue of Mansfield's possibly inconsistent philosophy about human nature: Do we have true selves or do we not? The question should never be asked of Mansfield, even though she may depict some characters who think one way and some who feel another. Mansfield does not know the answer either. The grandmother is what she is, and never mind how she got that way.

A few of Mrs. Fairfield's actions, however, do seem to require some interpretation, especially as they relate to her grandchild Kezia, who loves her and depends on her in much the same way young Kass Beauchamp loved her Granny Dyer (Alpers, 3). The first night in the new house, Kezia is waiting for her grandmother to come to bed, the last to do so in the household. As the grandmother gets into bed, she sighs. Kezia sticks her head under the old woman's arms and gives "a little squeak." Mansfield's description of the grandmother's response is noteworthy because two very minor words (*but* and *only*) are important keys to the grandmother's state of mind: "But the old woman only pressed her faintly, and sighed again, took out her teeth, and put them in a glass of water beside her on the floor" (*KM*, 231). These are sighs of resignation to her fate as a woman and to the need to do the things that must be done, such as taking good care of false teeth.

In the story "At the Bay," probably originally intended to serve as a second chapter in the novel that was never finished, Grandmother Fairfield again is forced by Kezia to sigh about things. Kezia asks her why she is "stopping and sort of staring at the wall?" (*KM*, 281). Following a paragraph that describes their setting and reads almost like stage directions, Kezia again asks why her grandmother seems so preoccupied. In response, "the old woman sighed, whipped the wool twice round her thumb, and drew the bone needle through" (*KM*, 282). Mansfield follows with a gem of a sentence that reflects the old woman's stoicism and serves as both a reflection of her attitude and an attitude toward her reflecting: "She was casting on," doing what she is here to do.

The grandmother, however, does tell Kezia what she has been thinking about: Kezia's dead Uncle William. Following a short discussion of Uncle William, Kezia asks her grandmother if thinking about him makes her sad, at which point Mansfield's story enters the grandmother's thought process: "Did it make her sad? To look back, back. To stare down the years, as Kezia had seen her doing. To look after *them* as a woman does, long after *they* were out of sight. Did it make her sad? No, life was like that" (*KM*, 282).

How does a reader interpret Mrs. Fairfield's view of life—as wisdom gained with age? as resignation forced on her by conditions she accepted? In truth, the interpretation must not be made at this point in the story, because the "act" involving Kezia and her grandmother is not yet finished. Kezia has yet to ask if everyone has to die. She responds vigorously to Mrs. Fairfield's statement that even Kezia will die someday: "What if I just won't? Mrs. Fairfield's response is to "sigh again" (with Mansfield calling direct attention to the act as occurring again) and to draw "a long thread from the ball" (*KM*, 283). Work must go on in this life, despite our need to sigh over it occasionally. This scene in "At the Bay" ends with Kezia tickling and kissing her grandmother in an effort to love her into promising never to die and leave Kezia alone. The old woman is finally forced to drop her knitting (put the practical work aside), to swing "back in the rocker" and begin "to tickle Kezia." They are "laughing in each other's arms" when Mrs. Fairfield proclaims, "Come, that's enough, my squirrel! That's enough, my wild pony! She sets "her cap straight" and commands Kezia to "pick up my knitting." The section of the story ends with the sentence "Both of them had forgotten what the 'never' was about" (*KM*, 283).

Life is like that. The young do not expect to die; the old have a resigned wisdom. The young are as natural as squirrels or wild ponies; the old can be tickled and loved into dropping their work for a few moments. And when we are in the act of truly loving each other, young and old, we are very likely to forget our demands to say *never, forever, always,* or any of the other words that cause individuals to box themselves into one condition that they then label life.

Mansfield most often uses her fictional techniques to go into the consciousness of a young woman struggling with her feelings of love and hate, with her emotions as a woman in a world clearly dominated by men, as we might well expect from a romantic, autobiographical writer who lived in such a world; however, the methods of objective characterization (both internal and external) that Mansfield began to develop in these two stories of the Burnell family helped her also to create other characters with equal verisimilitude. Understandable is Murry's appreciation of the words of one of his wife's printers: "But these kids are "*real!*" (*KM*, x).

Other stories that grew out of Mansfield's childhood in New Zealand include the very early story "New Dresses," the minor stories "The Little Girl" and "The Voyage," and the more significant "The Doll's House." ("New Dresses" is discussed later in Part 1 as one of several stories having a female-male theme.) "The Little Girl" is another Kezia story, one in which Kezia sees her father as "a figure to be feared and avoided." The sense of relief she feels every morning when he goes off to work foreshadows the freedom that comes on all the Burnell women when Stanley leaves for work in "At the Bay": "Oh, the relief, the difference it made to have the man out of the house. Their very voices were changed as they called to one another; they sounded warm and loving and as if they shared a secret" (*KM*, 270).

But if the characters and most of the emotions are the same in "The Little Girl" (first published in 1912) and "At the Bay" (published ten years later), the narrative technique is not. In "At the Bay" Mansfield has eliminated the first-person narrator of the earlier story but has not yet found her way into Kezia's mind in the manner she will later. The first sentence of "The Little Girl" reads, "To the little girl he was a figure to be feared and avoided" (*KM*, 138). That statement is clearly an external generalization about Kezia's attitudes and actions rather than an immediate opening leap into an ongoing action, as is the previously quoted beginning of *Prelude*: "There was not an inch of room for Lottie and Kezia."

The plot of "The Little Girl" concerns Kezia's innocently tearing

23

up her father's "great speech for the Port Authority" (*KM*, 140) to use for stuffing in the pincushion she is making for his birthday. Her hands are slapped with a ruler, causing her to sob, "What did Jesus make fathers for?" (*KM*, 141). Kezia's superficial observation of the five Macdonald children playing in the yard next door with their father causes her to decide that not all fathers are like hers, a conclusion that readers of Mansfield's stories may have trouble endorsing. This story, however, ends on what feminist critic Kate Fullbrook takes as a positive note, when Kezia, after a nightmare, is taken into her father's bed, because both her mother and her grandmother are out of the house, and discovers that, for cuddling, his body is harder than her grandmother's but is "a nice hardness." She begins to feel sorry for his having to go to work every day and being "too tired to be a Mr. Macdonald." The story ends with Kezia, her head resting on her father's chest, proclaiming, "What a big heart you've got, father dear" (*KM*, 142). Although Fullbrook finds the end sentimental, she approves of what Mansfield "is trying to do here," that is, to posit tentatively "a female sexuality whose basis is reflective, based on similarity rather than difference."[9]

Frankly, I have great difficulty being hopeful not about the actual existence of greater female-male rapprochement than has been thought possible in Western culture (largely by males and male psychologists such as Freud and Jung, as Fullbrook accurately charges) but about Mansfield's forecasting in her own time the possibility of such a coming together. Even more difficult to see is Mansfield's having opened "a new account of the links between male and female" (Fullbrook, 51). Rather, I read the sentimental conclusion of the story at face value, which is that the "funny feeling" that comes over Kezia because her father tells her to rub her feet against his legs for warmth is a deluded feeling rather than a revelatory one. The man is still gaining ascendancy through his ability to deliver physical comforts to the female. Hearing his heart beating is ironically a purely physical thing. Although little Kezia may equate "a big heart" with the ability to love another person, there is no evidence in this story or in later stories about Kezia's father that the action of the heart is transformed into actions of self-giving love. Mansfield's stories taken as a whole say that big and little girls who think well of men or who try to be their equals are in for rude awakenings—which is what Kezia may get in the morning from her father.

Probably the most interesting fact about "The Voyage" is that Mansfield apparently stopped working on "At the Bay" on 11 August 1921 in order to write the story in recognition of the third anniversary of her mother's death. The story merely recounts the boat trip of Grandmother Mary Crane and her granddaughter Fenella to Mrs. Crane's home, following the death of Fenella's mother. At home they find Grandfather Walter Crane in a huge bed, with just his silver-bearded face showing outside the covers. This element of the story may recapture (surely not from Mansfield's own memory) a boat trip in the writer's first year to visit her paternal grandparents. The father in this story, by the way, appears only briefly to see the travelers off. He sounds stern to Fenella but looks tired. He hugs his mother and says, "God bless you." When she returns that blessing and adds "my own brave son!" Fenella thinks, "This was so awful," and turns her back on them (*KM*, 526). Is this response to be read as a child's normal reaction to gushing adults or as a recognition of some falseness in the display of emotion? When Fenella asks her father how long she is going to stay at her grandmother's, he will not look at her. She is holding on to his lapels, but he shakes her off "gently." This depiction certainly seems to be another of those mixed views of a father, written by a daughter who had a confusing love/hate relationship with her own father.

In "The Doll's House," finished at the end of October 1922, Mansfield returns to the Burnells at a time that seems a few years later than that of the other stories about Kezia and her family. The story implies that they have been living in their house in the country for some time now, and Kezia, Lottie, and Isabel are all in school. There is no mention of a son; Father Stanley does not appear; Mother Linda utters but two sentences. "The Doll's House" is about the children—especially Kezia, who violates the family rules by inviting the outcast Kelvey girls to look at the wonderful dollhouse sent to the Burnell children by "dear old Mrs. Hay" (*KM*, 570), after a stay with the family. The fabulous dollhouse is the talk of the school, and the children are allowed to invite their school friends to come see it, though under terribly strict rules for children: no more than two at a time, just to look, not to stay to tea, not "to come traipsing through the house" (*KM*, 572), but to stand quietly in the courtyard admiring the little house as, the story implies, everyone should admire the Burnells and their big house.

Much scapegoating occurs in this story. The Burnells do not approve of the school to which the girls go, but there is no choice. They must

25

go and be mixed all together, the children of a judge, a doctor, a store-keeper, even a milkman; however, "the line" is drawn at the Kelveys, whose mother is a "hardworking little washer-woman" (*KM*, 573) and whose father is thought to be in jail. The children at school learn from their parents, taunting and teasing the Kelvey girls—Lil and our Else (she is always called that) Kelvey—in sport. One of the girls hisses at the Kelveys, "Yah, yer father's in prison!" These scapegoating words "deeply, deeply" excite all the other girls, who are so released from their own fears and limitations by heaping them on the Kelveys that they skip rope faster and harder, doing more "daring things" than they have ever done before (*KM*, 575).

One day Kezia, who is said only to have "made up her mind," speaks to the Kelvey girls and invites them to look at the dollhouse. Although Mansfield writes of Kezia's hesitation in inviting them, she offers nei-ther internal nor external reasons for Kezia's going against her mother's explicit orders. Lil, who is even more a victim of socialization than is Kezia, is afraid to accept the invitation, but our Else, who never speaks, implores with her eyes; thus, they go to look at the dollhouse. Descriptions of the Kelvey girls include their looking like "two little stray cats" and standing "still as a stone" (*KM*, 576). When Aunt Beryl discovers the invasion of her courtyard, she shoos the Kelveys out "as if they were chickens" (*KM*, 577). Later she thinks of them as rats. These images add up to the point that the adult Burnells do not even consider these little girls human. That Mansfield is depicting the psy-chology of scapegoating becomes even more obvious with an otherwise pointless paragraph about Aunt Beryl's feelings after she has chased the Kelveys away and shouted "bitterly" at Kezia, "Wicked, disobe-dient little girl." Aunt Beryl's "afternoon had been awful" because of a letter "from Willie Brent, a terrifying, threatening letter" that de-mands she meet him or expect a visit from him at her front door. Now, having "frightened those little rats of Kelveys and given Kezia a good scolding," Beryl's pain is lifted, the "ghastly pressure" is gone, and she can return to "the house humming" (*KM*, 577).

But our Else has the last word. The furnishing in the doll's house that Kezia loves most "frightfully" is a tiny lamp "in the middle of the dining-room table." Well out of sight of the Burnells, the Kelvey girls sit down to rest and our Else speaks her only words in the story: "I seen the little lamp" (*KM*, 577). Only Kezia in the Burnell family is capable of seeing and demonstrating the light of love—or human un-derstanding, compassion, or whatever a reader wants to call it.

That Mansfield found her new form by going back to the emotional days of her childhood attests to the great influence of that early time on her life; her feelings of love and hate for her parents were so mixed that only by giving them different shapes and names could she come to grips with them.

Female-Male Conflicts

As several of the stories of *In a German Pension* indicate, Mansfield began very early to write about love and female-male conflicts, both in and out of marriage. These topics remained among Mansfield's most consistently examined subjects during her short writing career. Of course, the joys and pains of love are a staple in the literary diet of most writers, and so what is important about the sexual conflicts in Mansfield's work is not their presence but their nature. What she says about love may be looked at for its consistency, to determine whether Mansfield depicts essentially the same kind of male-female relationship both over the course of her career and within stories about persons of various age and social groups. It is also appropriate, probably to a lesser extent, to examine how what Mansfield says about love relates to three elements: her own experiences of it, her milieu, and other fictional representations.

As noted previously, in *In a German Pension* Mansfield began very early to depict what Alpers has called "a fastidious feminine recoil from crudity" (112), though not exclusively from crudity of a sexual nature. One of the important issues in dealing with actions that women may "naturally" see as crude is to determine how much is natural in women collectively and how much is of societal origin. German gustatory crudity, which Mansfield depicts as existing in women and men (although the men seem to carry it to lower points), stands in clear contrast with the fastidiousness of the female narrator, but she is depicted as being English as well as female. And the Germans *do* make light of English manners in general. German wives *do* recoil from gross sexual acts that seem to result not in any pleasure for them but only in more children. Mansfield does not write about the physical pleasures, if any, that men receive from sexual intercourse. In fact, an examination of several stories about marriage and courtship will show that Mansfield almost never depicts the physicality of sex, a fact that stands in stark contrast with D. H. Lawrence's handling of sex in his fiction. Mansfield knew both Lawrence and his fiction well, but she was not terribly enamored of either, although probably affected by both.

Conflict in Marriages

In the clearly autobiographical early story "New Dresses," Anne and Henry Carsfield (a play on the writer's two family names, Beauchamp and Mansfield) have their differences. The Carsfields are obviously members of Mansfield's parents' generation. Henry returns home late one Saturday night to find Anne indulging herself in what he labels with obvious disgust as "moon-gazing." Her response is not a defense of her action but an attack on his: "My dear, how you smell of cigars!" He defends his smoking as necessary "with these other chaps," because he would look bad in refusing to smoke, although the reader is receiving no signals that Henry is more of a follower than a leader. Shortly, he calls Anne's attention to the moon "over there by the chimney," forgetting that just moments before he has accused her of doing what he now requires her to do. But Anne's moon gazing may have taken longer and been for purposes other than Henry's. He proclaims it a "fine night," a pronouncement that reminds him to tell Anne what he is proud of having done: making a "colossal joke," about which all his male friends shouted. Henry starts to tell her exactly what he said in response to another's saying, "Life is a game of cards" (*KM*, 28), but he stops and claims to have forgotten the exact words. Has he? Or do we credit him with realizing that words he could say to the men should not be repeated to Anne? He promises to remember the words later in bed. But before they get to bed, they continue what is clearly a running battle over expenses, which concludes but does not end with Mansfield's sentence "On and on stormed the voice" of Henry. Anne toils up to bed with her self-assuring thought that Henry will calm down when the "beer's worked off" (*KM*, 30).

In fact, Sunday dawns brilliantly with "Henry and Anne quite reconciled" (*KM*, 30) and Mansfield's having left it totally to her readers to imagine what events transpired in the bedroom overnight (assuming that Henry even got there) to reconcile the couple's immediate argument about current expenses, if not any basic differences between the characters themselves. The reader, by the way, never has to judge whether Henry's hilarious comment was indeed so splendid, because it is never told to his wife. By handling Henry's comment this way, Mansfield is able to imply his crudity without having to write it into her story.

The husband-wife conflict is not really the main concern of the story; it gains importance both because it is an indicator of Mansfield's constant awareness of the subject and because the ostensible main character is not fully realized. The Carsfields' daughter, Helen—another version of the young Kathleen Beauchamp—is the primary character in the story, or at least the plot line suggests that Mansfield meant her to be. Helen's tearing and throwing away her expensive new dress move the story along, and her peculiar nature (in the eyes of both her mother and her father) may seem to a reader to belong at the center of the story. Had they been more fully developed, Helen's personality and her conflict with her parents might have been more interesting than her parents and their difficulties with each other. The lack of focus on Helen and Mansfield's allowing her thematic concern with marital conflict to dominate the story mark "New Dresses" as an early work. In fact, despite the vivid argument between the adult Carsfields, this 1912 story falls off badly at the end. It concludes as kindly family physician Dr. Malcolm returns Helen's repaired dress to her grandmother in a scene that only satisfies plot information about the garment and does nothing about Helen's personality differing from family expectations, about her conflicts within the family, or about the continuing battle of the sexes between husband and wife.

If the early story "New Dresses" provides a look at what can be called a traditional marriage situation with a strong, demanding husband who goes to work and leaves children and all household duties to the weaker wife, then "Marriage à la Mode" (first published in December 1921) provides, even as the title says, a look at a different kind of marriage. Some of the elements are not changed, however; William still takes the train to the office, and Isabel stays home to care for the children, although "the children" this time are the several artistic and precious friends who mean much more to Isabel than do her husband and real children. William in this story is the more sensitive one, the one who is suffering, as opposed to the arrangement in "New Dresses," in which the woman fulfills that role.

Isabel is characterized in the first few paragraphs of the story with the word *new*. She laughs in a new way; she is the new Isabel; and William feels that he has lost the old Isabel, the one he married, who was exquisitely fresh (not new, though), like a "rose-bush, petal-soft, sparkling and cool" (*KM*, 556). Perhaps Mansfield's reference to the whole rosebush in contrast to Robert Burns's love that is like a "red, red rose" is meant to suggest the thorns in William's love.[10] The bulk of the story, taking place while William is home for one weekend, deals with the divine fellows and girls who are apparently sponging on Isabel and William. The couple has no last name, implying how far they have escaped from family and traditions, how free they are from the conventional. Everyone in this new world is on a first-name basis. William, however, finds relief from all this precious modernity by handling staid old legal documents on the train. When he gets back to London, he writes a letter to Isabel, who receives it the next day with the thought that it is *only* from William. In a display of her callousness toward him, she begins to read the letter to her friends; although she is pained in doing so, she reads through to the end, accompanied by such comments from her friends as "A love-letter! But how divine!" and "It's the most marvellous find." But when one of the friends asks Isabel for the letter to read it "mine own self" (*KM*, 563), Isabel crushes it and runs into the house. There she sees the truth about herself. Isabel believes that even "the grave bedroom knew her for what she was, shallow, tinkling, vain" (*KM*, 564). She wants to write to William, but her friends call from below. She honestly struggles with the question but finally tells herself that she can write to William later; thus, "laughing in the new way" (*KM*, 564), she runs down the stairs to her friends. By struggling with what to do, Isabel demonstrates that her real nature—her inborn qualities—may be at work.

Mansfield seems to portray a new Isabel, one who because of the modern environment has allowed herself to become "shallow, tinkling, vain." The distinction that Aristotle makes in his "Manichean Ethics" between an incontinent person and a self-indulgent one is equally at work in Mansfield's characterization of Isabel. She is incontinent: She, like the reader, knows the right thing to do (write to William), but she cannot do so, no matter how much she may want to. Were she merely self-indulgent, she would not even know that she should not be living this new life but would instead take for granted this new and liberated world. To assert that Isabel's inborn nature is at work in producing her incontinent behavior and her guilty conscience is to deny that she is merely still under the influence of an older, traditional environment in which women "learned" the right thing to do. The evidence to support this reading lies in the honest emotions Isabel expresses to herself about her treatment of William's letter. She calls her action "vile, odious, abominable, vulgar" (*KM*, 564). These emotions really do seem to come from her heart, not just from one set of older, nurtured responses that have been replaced by the new set of modern ones.

A much more successful and poignant story, this one about the failure of a husband to understand a wife, is "The Stranger." It treats not only a traditional marriage but apparently also Mansfield's own parents' marriage. Alpers says that the action recounted in "The Stranger" actually occurred between the Beauchamps and that Mansfield changed the site from Wellington to Auckland in the American edition of *The Garden Party and Other Stories* to ease her father's possible pain (361).

"The Stranger" is another of the relatively few stories told through a male consciousness that knows a good deal less about itself than the reader can perceive. Mr. Hammond, standing on the wharf awaiting the docking of the ship that is bringing his wife, Janey, home to New Zealand, is about as solipsistic as a human being can be. He believes that all the people on the wharf, even the workers, are as excited about Janey's arrival as he is. As Mansfield says, "he was so tremendously excited it never entered his head not to believe that this marvellous fact meant something to them too" (*KM*, 446). Because Mr. Hammond thinks the people are there to welcome Janey home, too, his heart warms toward them, they become a "decent" bunch, and the broad chests of the dockworkers even make him stick out his own chest in pride. At this point he immediately begins talking out loud, though not to any discernible person; nevertheless, at the end of his two-paragraph speech (it is not just plain talking) he manages to direct the whole discourse at Mr. Gaven, who has not previously been introduced into the story and is obviously just standing there, minding his own business and not, as Mr. Hammond assumes of everyone, Hammond's.

A subsequent episode with Jean Scott, the young daughter of two more persons there to greet the ship, suggests the possibility of John Hammond's being less self-centered and more concerned with others than he has seemed so far. But when he lifts Jean up onto a higher barrel, ostensibly so that the little girl can see better, Hammond may benefit more from the action than Jean does: "The movement of holding her, steadying her, relieved him wonderfully, lightened his heart" (*KM*, 448). When the delayed ship finally starts moving toward the dock, "Mr. Hammond has forgotten about Jean," as he springs away to focus all his nervous excitement on Captain Johnson, the harbormaster, offering him first a cigar, then two, and then the whole case. The emphasis on the cigars suggests the giving of cigars upon the birth of a baby and ought to be another warning to the reader that Hammond is going to suffer some change in his life, perhaps the introduction of a new or different life into his own. Earlier passing phrases have hinted that not all has been well in this marital relationship and that things may become worse (from Hammond's point of view, at least) in the future. He has imagined his wife having a cup of tea on board and himself "standing over her" (*KM*, 447).

A tremendous amount of possessiveness is conveyed in that single phrase. Hammond's high degree of nervousness during the long wait seems excessive for someone who is anticipating the arrival home of his loved one. This particular loved one is spotted at the rail and characterized in his mind by Hammond first as Janey and then immediately as Mrs. Hammond. In causing Hammond to think this way, Mansfield implies that he really does not understand his relationship with the woman, does not really know whether she is or should be thought of as Janey or Mrs. Hammond. Or perhaps he is less confused and more frightened by the possibility that the dependent Mrs. Hammond who went to Europe ten months ago will be the more independent Janey who returns. In either case, Hammond apparently has grounds for dreading what happens between him and Janey even before it happens in the story.

As the ship moves toward the dock, Hammond gets hold of himself, despite his shaking hands, and feels "able to face Janey" (*KM*, 449). Why should he not be able to face her? He again reveals his buried fear that something is going to be different in their relationship now that she has proved to both of them that she can function as Janey, on her own, and not just as Mrs. Hammond, under his watchful eye. When Hammond fails to complete his thought that Janey "had the courage of a—" (*KM*, 449), the reader may well want to supply the word that Hammond cannot say: *woman*. Mansfield's narrative technique of depicting what is occurring within Hammond's mind slowly reveals to the reader the reasons he thinks the way he does, without the author ever having to state those reasons directly.

As Mr. and Mrs. Hammond finally greet each other and John thinks in rapid-fire order that she is "just the same," "not a day changed," and "just as he'd always known her" (*KM*, 450), the reader becomes convinced that the stranger of the title is Janey Hammond, a stranger of some sort to John Hammond. When the "whole first-cabin" seems to want to say "good-bye to Janey," Hammond is bothered because of his desire to have her entirely to himself; still, he manages to relieve that minor misery by taking pride in her being "by far the most popular woman on board." Again he thinks of her as being the Janey he knows, "just her little self—just Janey all over: standing there with her veil thrown back" (*KM*, 451). At this point Mansfield seems to violate that subtle angle of narration that she has been weaving in this story: depicting John Hammond exclusively through his own words, thoughts, and eyes and seeing the surroundings only as he sees them. Two and a half sentences may seem to intrude: "Hammond never noticed what his wife had on. It was all the same to him whatever she wore. But to-day he did notice that she wore a black 'costume'—didn't they call it?—with white frills, trimmings, he supposed they were at the neck and sleeves" (*KM*, 451).

The first two sentences of this quoted passage appear to come from an outside consciousness; it seems highly unlikely that Hammond would think here about his not knowing what his wife wears most of the time. Moreover, the language is not what he would use in having such a thought. But then in the third sentence this external observation and evaluation of Hammond fades out; his consciousness returns in the words *black "costume"* and remains present not only for the remainder of the passage, but probably for the rest of the story. Taking the attitude of a New Critic, one would have to say that this shift in narrative voice is a blemish on the art object, which is assumed by the romantic writer and critic to be seeking an ideal unity. Most real readers of the story, however, probably pass right through this passage without noticing that anything has happened differently. The needed factual information is conveyed. Only in examining the story line by line in anticipation of such a "blemish" can a New Critic discover that one actually does occur. What this shift in narrative voice does to the story may be of less importance than what it does for the ego of the critic who discovers it, thereby winning a victory over an art object that has ostensibly presented itself in advance as perfect.

Meanwhile, Hammond has been suffering another blow to his expectations. Janey has gone to say good-bye to the ship's doctor and has clearly not wanted John to accompany her. Naturally, he thinks she is "keeping something from him." Accordingly, he begins to have reservations about the very words and actions that have just moments before reflected the real Janey. Now he thinks that "he'd noticed just something. She was just a touch too calm—too steady" (*KM*, 452). If Hammond is prevented from seeing the real Janey because of his overweening need to possess the kind of woman he thinks he deserves, Janey can see *him* quite clearly. She makes him stand still for observation, commenting on his trimmed beard and thinner look, ending with the remark that "Bachelor life agrees with you" (*KM*, 452). Of course, he objects to that comment and catches her close to him, feeling "again, as always" that he is "holding something that never was quite his—his" (*KM*, 453). Perhaps that strange-looking "his—his" construction can be completed by such missing phrases as these: *his wife—his to possess*. It should be increasingly clear in the story that Hammond's great need is to possess his wife entirely, to make her a mere extension of himself. And so when he subsequently says to her in their hotel room—where he anticipates staying overnight, rather than immediately heading home to the children—"I feel I'll never have you to myself again" (*KM*, 454), the reader is supposed to believe that he has never had her to himself. Janey wants to read the children's letters that John has brought with him, but because John believes he cannot afford to lose her to them, either, he insists she read the letters later. Finally agreeing to do so, she tucks the letters into her blouse, putting the children symbolically closer to her heart than John has probably ever been. Going contrary to everything he has hoped for from this reunion, the relationship moves out of his control.

To try to get it back, to try "to make Janey so much part of him that there wasn't any of her to escape" (*KM*, 455), John blushingly requests that she kiss him. Mansfield makes no statement about how Hammond says, "Kiss me, Janey! You kiss me!" (*KM*, 455). Thus every reader must decide how Hammond would say those two sentences. Is he closer to pleading or to commanding? In any case, "there was a tiny pause," just long enough "for him to suffer torture," and then Janey kisses him "as she always kissed him, as though the kiss—how could he describe it?—confirmed what they were saying, signed the contract." This kind of perfunctory kiss is not "at all what he thirsted for" (*KM*, 455–56).

At this point a reader may actually begin to sympathize to some degree with Hammond, but the degree may well depend on how that reader interprets John's asking Janey to kiss him. The reader at the pleading end of the spectrum may have a great deal more sympathy than the one who sees John as commanding a kiss. As in all such matters, trained or indoctrinated twentieth-century readers have come to expect a consistency of characterization to which they can consistently respond. The reader who is beginning to sympathize with John's "reasonable," or at least understandable, desire for his wife to love him passionately will certainly question her motives in telling John the story about why the ship was delayed in making port—because a young man had died the night before. John has not asked Janey anything about the delay of the ship, although while it was occurring earlier he was much agitated about it. Janey may have some personal need to tell the story about the man's death, which occurred in her arms with the two of them absolutely alone. These facts cause her husband almost to have a heart attack himself and to think of himself: "What was she doing to him! This would kill him!" (*KM*, 456). Surely Janey's telling John about this event may involve some degree of hubris on her part; she does seem to take pride in the fact that she was the person who comforted the dying man.

Likewise, she may be telling the story to John in order to demonstrate to him that she really is a compassionate and loving woman. If so, she is certainly rubbing salt in his emotional wounds, in effect saying to him that "I *can* love, so if I do not demonstrate it to you, it is because something is wrong with you rather than with me." This interpretation of Janey's motives can be reinforced by observing her response when John asks her why the stewardess did not serve as comforter to the dying man: "'Oh, my dear—the stewardess!' said Janey. 'What would he have felt?'" (*KM*, 457). Janey's tender feelings for her fellow passenger on the ship do not seem to extend equally to her husband. Surely she must know John well enough to realize that this story is going to hurt him deeply. It almost seems as if she tells him about it deliberately to hurt him. Other than to receive praise for her own actions or to hurt him, a reader at this point may see no need for Janey ever to tell John anything about the episode. Janey's callousness or her devastating naïveté seems to come out when, in the face of his obvious display of great pain, she says, "You're not—sorry I told you, John darling? It hasn't made you sad? It hasn't spoilt our evening—our being alone together?" (*KM*, 458). Of course it has, and so John buries his face in her bosom, with his arms around her, and thinks, to end the story, "Spoilt their evening! Spoilt their being alone together! They would never be alone together again" (*KM*, 458).

Probably the Hammonds have never been "alone together," or—even more accurately, to play on Mansfield's beautifully chosen words—each one of them has always been alone every time they have been together. They are severely mismatched. Neither receives a needed kind of love from the other. A story that begins with John looking very much like the only source of his own misery because he demands things of his wife that she cannot possibly give concludes with Janey sharing the blame for torturing John with a story about how she can give more of herself to a stranger than she has ever given to him. If we can credit Janey with not really knowing that her story will hurt John, then we can enjoy the triple play of the title, in which there are three strangers. Blame for their failure to love each other can certainly be shared, if *blame* is the right word; can either be blamed for not being what the other needs? If Janey is a stranger to John, can we say that he is an equal stranger to her? The story does not seem to read that way. She seems to have much more knowledge about what hurts him and to hurt him willfully. John is obviously self-centered and demanding, but Mansfield's subtle portrayal of Janey makes her at first seem to be a less sympathetic character than the bare circumstances of the event might suggest.

Only at the conclusion of the story can a reader come to an understanding of why Janey tells John about the shipboard incident. She knows exactly what she is doing and why she does it, which is to create a situation that may make John admit first to himself and then to her that their marriage is not going well. John's horror that they will "never be alone together again" indicates that he is not picking up her signal, and so the reader's expectation probably is that the marriage will continue in much the same vein. In fact, Mansfield's overall portrayal of such traditional marriages as those of the Hammonds, Burnells, and Sheridans is that they have to be continued for social and religious reasons despite whatever unhappiness the partners (perhaps largely the women) may be suffering.

Even though "The Stranger" never enters Janey's mind and all her words and actions are filtered through John's consciousness, Mansfield's magical handling of point of view makes it possible for the reader to know things about the Hammonds' marriage that both Janey and John secretly know, but only Janey is willing to bring to the surface. John has probably been seeing the real Janey for a long time, but he has never been able to admit to himself that she is something other than what he needs to believe she is. By telling him how she nursed this other man, Janey, in effect, says to John, "I am not what you think I am and what you so desperately need me to be." The key to this interpretation lies, however, in Janey's actual first two questions of John as she gets off the ship: "Well, darling! Have you been waiting long? How are the children, John?" (*KM*, 450).

Yes, he has been waiting a long time, as she has too, for real satisfaction in marriage, and the children (about whom John thought, "Hang the children," when she asked of them) are the only result of their marriage that matters and the main factor that may keep these two strangers together.

"The Stranger" has often been compared favorably with James

Joyce's "The Dead," primarily for the shared theme: A self-important, strong husband is made aware of his wife's ability to love another.[11] Yet the interpretation made here—in which Janey must share the responsibility with John for their inability to love each other selflessly—separates Mansfield's story from Joyce's. Nothing in "The Dead" remotely suggests that Gretta in any way needs to hurt Gabriel in telling him about her long-ago love for Michael Furey. Although "The Dead" had been in print for some six years in *Dubliners* when Mansfield wrote her story, Alpers sees no evidence that she had ever read it (330). And despite the common imagery of cold and snow that appears close to the end of both stories to designate the emotional feelings of each husband, Mansfield's story cannot reasonably be viewed as owing anything to Joyce's. In fact, the differences in the two seem to be of greater significance than their similarities.

Another story that deals with a woman's attempt to alter her marital relationship is "A Cup of Tea," written in four or five hours on 11 January 1922, almost exactly a year before Mansfield died (*KM, Journal,* 284). The actual wife-husband conflict here does not surface until the end of the story, where it creates the resolution. Told through a narrative voice that at the beginning seems to be chatting with a given listener, the story settles down after a baffling start into a fairly standard Mansfield version of a tale in which an omniscient narrator tells the story about half the time in the words the characters would have used had they been allowed to speak directly, rather than having their thoughts expressed through indirect discourse.

To open the story, Rosemary Fell is described—in the witty, sophisticated, just slightly jaded tone that some Mansfield critics do not like too much—as being "not exactly beautiful" but "brilliant," "well read," "well dressed," and capable of achieving "the most delicious mixture of the really important people" at her parties (*KM,* 584). Rosemary sounds at first much like Isabel of "Marriage à la Mode," a story published less than two weeks before "A Cup of Tea" was written. The first four sentences of the second paragraph probably perplex most readers: "Rosemary had been married two years. She had a duck of a boy. No, not Peter—Michael. And her husband absolutely adored her" (*KM,* 584). The sentence about what are apparently her two sons, Peter and Michael, seems directly aimed at some listener who knows the names of these two boys and has somehow indicated to the narrator that Peter, rather than Michael, is the "duck of a boy."

Actually, which boy is being described seems to make no difference to the rest of the story; in fact, what happens in the story in no way involves the boys. The narrator's apparent recognition of the presence of an active and responsive but nonspeaking audience is somewhat like what happens in Robert Browning's dramatic monologues. One other sentence near the beginning of the story makes use of a general second-person pronoun, but the effect of this sentence is quite different from the sudden intrusion just cited: "But if Rosemary wanted to shop she would go to Paris as you and I would go to Bond Street" (*KM*, 584). That sentence implies an audience much less strongly than the one about the boys does. The primary action of the story sounds as if it occurs two years after Rosemary's marriage, a point at which it is possible but not likely that she has borne two sons. Nonetheless, the narrator could be telling the story quite some time after its occurrence and wanting to make certain that the listener knows the boy being described as "a duck" is Michael, the first child, and not Peter, the second.

If these observations represent a reasonable reading of the textual material, they still do not explain why the boys are mentioned at all. One possibility is that the reference to a second child, who must have come later, demonstrates that the marriage has been consummated at least once more after this episode in Rosemary's life. Because the endurance of the marriage is made questionable by the actions of both Rosemary and her husband, Philip, the mentioning of the second child may mean that the condition described in the next sentence—"And her husband absolutely adored her" (*KM*, 584)—obtains at least up to the time of the telling of this story, which is at some indeterminate point past its occurrence. My analysis shortly will suggest that Philip adores his wife but may not "love" her as she needs to be loved. Mansfield critic Saralyn Daly has aptly described Rosemary as "artificial, idle, insensitive" and has called the narrator's tone malicious, intended by Mansfield to indicate that Rosemary's behavior "deserves no compassion."[12] Perhaps Mansfield needs compassion from a reader trying to make sense of this puzzling beginning.

The story proper is about how Rosemary, while out shopping one rainy winter afternoon, is asked by "a young girl, thin, dark, shadowy" to give her "the price of a cup of tea." Rosemary's response is suddenly to see the possibility of "an adventure," "like something out of a novel by Dostoevsky" (*KM*, 586). She thinks how thrilling it will be to take the girl home with her, and so she invites the girl to tea. Despite the latter's reluctance to go and her expressed fear that Rosemary may be taking her to a police station, Rosemary prevails. As they drive to Rosemary's home, Rosemary's thoughts are conveyed indirectly by the narrator and provide an example of the kind of malicious tone that Daly might have cited: "[Rosemary] had a feeling of triumph as she slipped her hand through the velvet strap [of the auto]. "She could have said, 'Now I've got you,' as she gazed at the little captive she had netted. But of course she meant it kindly. Oh, more than kindly. She was going to prove to this girl that—wonderful things did happen in life, that— fairy godmothers were real, that—rich people had hearts, and that women *were* sisters" (*KM*, 587).

These thoughts, if rather unrealistic, are not obviously malicious. The maliciousness lies not in what Rosemary is doing but in the reasons she is giving herself for doing it. If Rosemary deserves any compassion from a reader (and Daly says she does not), it will be because of an understanding of the real reasons she feels compelled to take this girl home—reasons no reader can possibly know at this point in the story. Compassion will come, if at all, only when the whole story is known. Right now, Rosemary is doing a malicious thing and having malicious thoughts; the narrator is not at fault.

"Longing to begin to be generous" (*KM*, 587), probably because she never has been before and perhaps because she carries unacknowledged guilt from her husband's excessive generosity toward her, Rosemary hurries the girl upstairs to her bedroom. The significance of Rosemary's choosing to have tea in her bedroom and of deciding, on the way there, not to ring for her maid but to "take off her things by herself" is probably not grasped at this point by most readers. Rosemary's thought that "the great thing was to be natural" (*KM*, 588) may arouse suspicion about her desires, because the word *her* in "take off her things" can refer to either woman. Besides, little about this whole episode seems natural. By causing Rosemary to think about being natural, Mansfield reinforces the abnormality, unnaturalness, and perhaps sickness of what Rosemary is doing for the reasons she is doing it— again, reasons the reader cannot yet know, despite realizing that they are (to Rosemary) bad reasons, whatever they may be. Naturally, the girl is frightened and has to be "half pushed" into a chair, where she sits motionless. At this point another disturbing narrative sentence enters: "To be quite sincere, [the girl] looked rather stupid" (*KM*, 588). This is an unlikely thought for Rosemary to have; it too reads as if the narrator is addressing that immediate listening audience predicated at the beginning of the story.

Rosemary finally gets the outer garments off the girl, but the girl threatens to faint, almost cries out for nourishment, and bursts into tears. The moment is described as "terrible and fascinating," apparently to Rosemary, who kneels beside the chair. The following two paragraphs imply that both women are moved by what is happening, with the word *moved* meaning that their attitudes shift, something changes:

> "Don't cry, poor little thing," [Rosemary] said. "Don't cry." And she gave the other her lace handkerchief. She really was touched beyond words. She put her arm round those thin, birdlike shoulders.
>
> Now at least the other forgot to be shy, forgot everything except that they were both women, and gasped out: "I can't go on no longer like this. I can't bear it. I shall do away with myself. I can't bear no more." (*KM*, 589)

The honest, perhaps even natural language of both women calls for compassion for Rosemary as much as for the girl, and the bid for the reader's understanding of Rosemary continues as she promises to look after the girl, to "arrange something." The reader's sympathy, however, cannot remain unalloyed, for Rosemary may in fact be back to "normal," for her, when she says they will have tea "and you'll tell me everything" (*KM*, 589). Just simply feeding this hungry girl will not satisfy Rosemary's need to have a thrilling experience; she needs to know the worst that happens to persons from the other side. When she demands that the girl stop crying because "it's so exhausting," she is concerned not with the girl's exhaustion but with her own, unless, of course, the girl may become so exhausted that she cannot tell Rosemary her story. This interpretation of Rosemary's motives behind her own seeming display of compassion is reinforced when, after the girl has eaten and is marvelously changed by "that slight meal," Rosemary lights "a fresh cigarette" and thinks "it was time to begin" (*KM*, 589).

And so the first question Rosemary asks is when the girl had her last meal, a question whose answer from the lower depths will thrill Rosemary actually as the Russian novelists do vicariously. But before the girl can reply and begin to pay dearly for her "slight meal," the door opens and husband Philip comes in to be introduced to the girl, who alleges her name is Smith.

Part 1

The arrival of Philip on the scene and the effect he has on Rosemary demonstrate that Rosemary's need to pick up this girl is closely connected to her relationship with her husband. Although he may adore her and be so rich that she can buy almost anything she wants, Philip does not satisfy some emotional needs in Rosemary's life. They politely excuse themselves from Miss Smith to go to the library to discuss—rationally and perhaps among non-Russian books—what exactly is going on. When Philip asks Rosemary "what on earth" she is "going to do with" the girl, Rosemary's stammering, incomplete reply that she is going to "be nice to her" and "show her—treat her—make her feel" probably says more about the incomplete and unsatisfying relationship she has with Philip than about what she expects to get from or give to this girl. Philip replies that whatever it is that Rosemary supposes she wants to do cannot be done, "it simply can't be done" (*KM*, 590). Philip stamps himself here with the mark of a traditional, rational, sexually repressed male who undoubtedly has said many times before to Rosemary's unclear and never fully articulated emotional and physical requests that they "simply can't be done." When Rosemary responds, "I knew you'd say that," she informs the reader that Philip always puts the quietus on Rosemary's need to do things because they are the sorts of things done in Russian novels. Because she does not manage to complete this thrilling episode with the girl, Rosemary still does not know, at the conclusion of the story, how she might actually respond to an emotional experience like the ones she has read about.

A reader might very well be left, at the end, with the impression that Rosemary will need to continue to pursue such experiences until one finally does catch up with her. Perhaps the encounter will be devastating to Rosemary. Perhaps she already knows that, which may be why she so easily gives in to Philip's demand (not phrased as one, of course) to send Miss Smith away.

Clearly not wanting to appear totally dictatorial, Philip speaks "slowly," thinking about what approach to take, while he cuts "the end of a cigar," an action with a phallic connotation that seems to have upside-down symbolic values: Philip is cutting off not his own sexual satisfactions, restrained though they may be, but those of Rosemary. The ploy that he hopes will get this wild plan out of Rosemary's head is to tell her that the girl is "astonishingly pretty." It works: "'Pretty?' Rosemary was so surprised that she blushed. 'Do you think so? I—I hadn't thought about it'" (*KM*, 590).

Why should Rosemary blush? One possible reason in this extremely complicated and interesting emotional relationship created by Mansfield is that Rosemary is made to realize that she really has been physically attracted to Miss Smith and that their future relationships, so ambiguously grasped by Rosemary, might well follow a lesbian route; after all, Rosemary is being cut off from her husband's phallus. Less likely, Rosemary may blush simply because she is made to realize that even in her "exquisitely well dressed" state she is not as pretty in her husband's eyes as Miss Smith is in her bedraggled condition. Neither of these readings, of course, speaks to the issue of whether Miss Smith is or is not pretty by anyone's standards. Narrative descriptions of her leave the question open. Philip achieves his objective by saying she is, thereby upsetting Rosemary, who may have equal fears about her own and her husband's potential sexual involvement with Miss Smith.

Philip keeps the pressure on Rosemary, proclaiming the girl "absolutely lovely" and asserting that he "was bowled over" when he entered the bedroom. The narrative description of Philip's response at the time does little to either support or deny this later description; the earlier passage merely states that Philip "stopped and stared." While telling his wife how beautiful the girl is, Philip strikes a match, apparently to light his cigar, although the story does not say that. Again, this symbolic action may have a number of values, ranging from the sexual to notions about the bringing of light—or even sending Rosemary's plans up in smoke. However a reader may interpret the symbolism, certainly Philip's action is self-centered, casual, unperturbed, that of a man completely in control, a man who knows that he has won this little contest and can smoke his victory cigar.

When Rosemary leaves the library, she goes to her writing room, where she first thinks of writing a check to Miss Smith but then decides it would be better to give the girl cash, drawing out five one-pound notes but then putting two back. After all, why should she pay too much for a thrilling story she never got? Before deciding how to compensate Miss Smith for her own bad conscience and confusion, Rosemary forcefully thinks to herself: "Pretty! Absolutely lovely! Bowled over. Her heart beat like a heavy bell. Pretty! Lovely!" (*KM*, 591).

Demonstrating to readers that both Rosemary and Philip are finished with Miss Smith and that the latter has completed her role in this domestic struggle, Mansfield writes nothing about what happens when Rosemary pays her off. The story jumps forward a half hour, to when Philip is still calmly waiting in the library, smoking his cigar, we may assume, but definitely reading the newspaper—suggesting both his lack of nervousness about the event and the fact that he gets his stories from less thrilling sources than his wife does. Rosemary, in that half hour, has dispatched Miss Smith and "done her hair, darkened her eyes a little, and put on her pearls" (*KM*, 591), girding for battle, as it were.

The initial words between Rosemary and Philip are designed by both to show how emotionally sophisticated they are, how little this Smith affair really matters. As Rosemary looks at Philip "with her dazzled exotic gaze" and leans "against the door," she says, "I only wanted to tell you" that "Miss Smith won't dine with us tonight." Philip responds, "Oh, what's happened? Previous engagement?" Sitting down on Philip's knee, Rosemary tells him she has given "the poor little thing" some money (the amount is not revealed to Philip) because "I couldn't keep her against her will, could I?" She touches Philip's cheeks with both hands and asks him, "Do you like me?" Her tone, described by Mansfield as "sweet, husky," troubles Philip, who, while holding her "tighter," says, "I like you awfully." Then, resembling John Hammond in "The Stranger," Philip says, "Kiss me." The story reads, "There was a pause." Apparently there is no kiss; rather, Rosemary says "dreamily, 'I saw a fascinating little box today. It cost twenty-eight guineas. May I have it?'" Jumping her on his knee, Philip says, "You may, little wasteful one." Then the story ends this way: "But that was not really what Rosemary wanted to say, 'Philip,' she whispered, and she pressed his head against her bosom, 'am I *pretty?*'" (*KM*, 591).

"A Cup of Tea" is solely about the woman's needs and desires. Unlike "The Stranger," in which the needs and emotions of both characters are on display and a reader may hold degrees of sympathy for both, "A Cup of Tea" places no importance on Philip's emotional condition. In fact, we can merely conjecture about Philip's motives and feelings toward Rosemary. He says that he likes her "awfully," but what about her he likes is not at all clear. Her "sweet, husky" tone of voice troubles him, but the reader can only guess that he is troubled by the hints of real sexuality in that voice. He asks Rosemary to kiss him, a good sign, but she does not do so, a bad one. In allowing her to buy the little box and almost anything else she wants, Philip indulges Rosemary almost as if she were a child. In fact, Philip at least twice uses words that place his wife into more of a child's category: He calls her "my darling girl" and insists she "look again, my child," at Miss Smith's alleged beauty. Rosemary's modern, well-dressed appearance and her socially important parties may be all that Philip requires of a wife, except, of course, for the male heirs, of which she has perhaps produced two. These conjectures about the nature of Philip's emotional needs and reasons for being married to Rosemary are relatively unimportant in the face of "A Cup of Tea" being Rosemary's story.

Clearly, Rosemary needs love. Perhaps she needs it with Miss Smith. She does not need more boxes, but if that is all she can get, she will have to take them. Rosemary's hesitance in buying this particular box in the first place should not be dismissed as merely an effort to save a little of her husband's money; rather, it should be seen as a realization on her part that the box on this particular shopping trip is not going to satisfy her. As she demonstrates with Miss Smith immediately after leaving the shop, where Rosemary asked in a "dreamy" voice that the box be held for her, she needs something other than another material possession. She needs something as badly as Miss Smith needs a cup of tea. An exceedingly telling trio of sentences occurs in Rosemary's mind in between her leaving the shop and being accosted by the hungry girl: "There are moments, horrible moments in life, when one emerges from shelter and looks out, and it's awful. One oughtn't to give way to them. One ought to go home and have an extra-special tea" (*KM*, 586).

Rosemary has just emerged from the shelter of her heterosexual marriage and her material possessions, but she does give way to her yearnings for something else when the girl suddenly presents the opportunity for Rosemary to "go home" for a tea that may be so "extra-special" that she cannot really handle it. Perhaps she actually welcomes Philip's breaking it up, even if for his own selfish reasons. At the end of the story, Rosemary is, at least for the moment, saved from her need to do "something out of a novel by Dostoevsky" and acquiesces to being boxed into a rich English society, so long as her husband, in addition to adoring her and liking her awfully, will just occasionally tell her she is *pretty*.

Conflicts in Courtship

In addition to depicting both modern and traditional marriages, Mansfield presents courtship stories that reveal similar conflicts between the sexes. "Mr. and Mrs. Dove" is a 1921 story indicating that getting into a marriage may be almost as painful as staying in one. Although Mansfield said that "Mr. and Mrs. Dove" is "not quite the kind of truth I'm after," because it is "a little bit made up" and "not inevitable" in its outcome, the story has considerable merit for its depiction of the psychologies of the two young people engaged in what the author called "this wretched cat and mouse act" (*KM, Journal*, 256).

One of the minority of Mansfield's stories told through a male consciousness, the story begins with one of those tantalizing paragraphs indirectly within the mind of the protagonist, a paragraph in which the character knows exactly what he is thinking about but the reader must enjoy a slow revelation of where the train of thought is leading. Reggie (would that name have connoted a weak male in 1921 England as it does in the United States some seventy years later?) is bemoaning his chances of success in asking Colonel Proctor for permission to marry his daughter Anne. Reggie estimates his personal and financial status and finds that even from the most objective view he has no chance of winning Anne's hand, but "so terrific" is his love for her that he resolves to go to the Proctor home and "try my luck" (*KM*, 498). Even before he gets away from his own home, however, his luck suffers a setback because his widowed, domineering mother is out in the garden snipping the heads off flowers, a symbolic action that Reggie understands: "Poor little beggars; they were getting it!" (*KM*, 499). Although "mater" demands to know where he is going, he escapes without telling her.

At the Proctors, only Anne is at home. The traditional, Victorian nature of their courtship is evident in Reggie's consternation when Anne tells him, "There's only me to entertain you, Reggie" (*KM*, 500). He can only state that he has come to say good-bye before he returns to his inherited fruit farm in Rhodesia. At this point Anne laughs at Reggie, "a long, soft peal," for which she quickly apologizes, saying that she has a "bad ha-habit" and does not know why she always laughs at him. Because Mansfield has also given Anne the other bad habit of stuttering ever so slightly (the insinuations of it are scattered and lightly suggestive), the reader is invited to interpret Anne's habit of laughing at Reggie as being similar in some way to her stuttering. Because stuttering is a natural occurrence in many persons' speech patterns made worse and "habitual" in some individuals as a result of psychological pressure not to stutter, Anne's laughing at Reggie can therefore be seen as taking a similar form. Her laughing is a natural reaction to him made worse by her efforts not to do it, because she knows that it hurts him. Looked at this way, Reggie seems to be a character who is naturally to be laughed at. He is a laughable character, by nature. Anne is less to blame for the laughing than Reggie is, but he cannot help being what he is—laughable. This interpretation is supported by Reggie's statement following Anne's apology for laughing: "I love to hear you laughing! I can't imagine anything more—" (*KM*, 500).

Whatever Reggie's unfinished sentence might have conveyed in the way of a soothing message, he apparently knows it to be a lie, because the narration abruptly returns to his consciousness for this interesting, unspoken alternate message: "But the truth was, and they both knew it, she wasn't always laughing; it wasn't really a habit" (*KM*, 500). Does Mansfield intend for Reggie's thought to stand as an objective, truthful evaluation of the situation? Because it is clearly in his mind, clearly his interpretation of Anne's laughing and of their relationship, it cannot be read as objective, even though a too-hasty reading of the sentence might make it seem so. But just because it is not objective does not mean that it is not true. In fact, at this point in the story a reader should not stand convinced in any direction about the truth or falsity of Reggie's evaluation. The evidence about Anne and Reggie's relationship is accumulating, but it is not complete. What Reggie does believe about it all can be determined: He believes that Anne is not a habitual laugher, as she is a habitual stutterer; he believes that she laughs only at him. This interpretation seems compatible with the earlier assertion that Reggie is a laughable person.

When Anne insists that Reggie sit down and invites him to smoke and to give her a cigarette, too, the action means more to the story than simply giving the couple more time to talk before he leaves. The reader needs to remember that at the beginning of the story Reggie did not smoke in his own bedroom because "mater hated" his doing that. If nothing else, the contrast suggests that Anne cares more about Reggie's doing things he likes than his mother does; then again, she may want to smoke and can hardly do so without inviting him first. While they are smoking together and talking about his emotions in returning to Rhodesia, the sounds of cooing come to them from Anne's pair of doves on the veranda. The birds (called Mr. and Mrs. Dove) should remind the reader of the pair of Pekes in the garden with mater when Reggie left to come to the Proctors and should therefore create another point of comparison between mater and Anne. Furthermore, the Pekes are connected to mater in a way that resembles Reggie's own connection to his "grim parent." Reggie's earlier mental description of the Pekes is important: "Biddy lay down with her tongue poked out;

she was so fat and glossy she looked like a lump of half-melted toffee. But Chinny's porcelain eyes gloomed at Reginald, and he sniffed faintly, as though the whole world were one unpleasant smell" (*KM*, 499). Reggie gives no indication that he equates this pair of dogs with old married couples, with how he and Anne may be at some future date. Nor is the reader encouraged at this point to make such a comparison. But later, when Anne obviously interprets the actions of Mr. and Mrs. Dove as paralleling those of herself and Reggie, the reader is almost forced to look at the Pekes in a new light.

Reggie finally does it, gets it over with, asking Anne if she thinks she could ever care for him. She replies, "No, never in that way" (*KM*, 502). There follows on the part of both characters much honest soul-searching, in which Mansfield is as good as she ever is at depicting the obfuscating, psychologically significant words and actions of characters who have little real idea of what they are doing. Earlier, Reggie has thought to himself that he "wished to God he understood" his and Anne's relationship. A reader might well echo Reggie's wish and might make the same evaluation that Mansfield did about its being a cat-and-mouse game. Anne counters Reggie's assertion that she laughs at him because she is "so far above" him "in every way," by saying that he is really a much better person than she is, calling him "marvellously un-selfish," and "kind and simple," and asserting that she is "none of those things" (*KM*, 503). Silencing Reggie's apparent attempt to protest, Anne says that this comparison of virtues and weaknesses is "not the point" anyhow.

The point is, as Anne puts it, that "I couldn't possibly marry a man I laughed at. Surely you see that. The man I marry—" (*KM*, 503). She removes her hand from Reggie's, smiles "strangely, dreamily," and repeats her unfinished sentence. It's all very dramatic, with a staged quality, a perception reinforced by Reggie's imagining the kind of man Anne can marry: one they had "seen often at the theater, walking on to the stage from nowhere, without a word, catching the heroine in his arms." Mansfield writes that Reggie bows "to his vision" and says, "Yes, I see." Anne's questioning response, "Do you?" (*KM*, 503) should probably also be the reader's. Does Reggie indeed see what Anne really wants? Does Anne herself know what she really wants? She says she has never known anyone she likes more than she likes Reggie: "I've never felt so happy with any one. But I'm sure it's not what people and what books mean when they talk about love" (*KM*, 503). It might seem at this point that the story is no more than another look at a silly romantic girl who, because of her book-induced notions of what love is supposed to mean, will reject a man who really loves her.

Yet the presence of the two pairs of pets and the way the story ends raise more questions about human nature than about romantic love, which, of course, may also be a manifestation of some portion of human nature. The story concludes with Reggie wanting to leave, to get away from the blow he received when Anne called the possibility of their marrying "fatal," wrong, and even "wicked" and then added "I mean, it's all very well for Mr. and Mrs. Dove. But imagine that in real life— imagine it" (*KM*, 504). Reggie agrees, "Oh, absolutely," but unhappiness is written so clearly on his face that Anne, "to his astonishment, this time, instead of laughing," looks like a little girl about to cry. When Reggie insists that he must "cut off now," Anne goes from nearly crying to scorn, anger, and a crimson face, stamping her foot and shouting at Reggie, "How can you be so cruel? I can't let you go until I know for certain that you are just as happy as you were before you asked me to marry you. Surely you must see that, it's so simple" (504). "But," the passage continues, "it did not seem at all simple to Reginald. It seemed impossibly difficult" (*KM*, 505).

And so it must seem to the reader who is trying to make sense of Anne's actions, to understand her motives and intentions. She again blames herself, saying, "It's all my fault." To these words Reggie objects, saying "It's just fate." He nearly runs in his haste to escape; the doves coo; Anne calls his name; and he stops and looks back at her "timid, puzzled" face and hears her "little laugh." The story closes with Anne saying, "Come back, Mr. Dove," and the sentence "And Reginald came slowly across the lawn" (*KM*, 505). Of course, the simplistic emotional reaction of many of Mansfield's contemporary readers brought up to look for happy endings (remember, this is still 1921) is that Reggie and Anne went on to marry and to coo at each other like Mr. and Mrs. Dove and that such a marriage is a naturally good thing. The ending of the story allows for that interpretation, but the totality of the story belies such a reading. If that reaction is all there is to the story, then it is little more than another romantic fairy tale. Even if Mansfield in writing the story did not manage to convey "quite the kind of truth" she was after, she conveyed something more than the feeling that Anne and Reggie married and cooed happily ever after.

Reggie's thought that their relationship is not "at all simple" but "impossibly difficult" applies not just to an interpretation of the relationship but also to any analysis of how Mansfield achieves her effects in the story. These complex short stories can no more be fully explained than poetry can be paraphrased. Looking again at the Pekes and the doves may help in this partial analysis. Reggie thinks of the dogs in somewhat human terms: Biddy is fat and happy; Chinny is gloomy and knows that the world smells bad. But Reggie draws no conclusions from this observation; he makes no judgment about how the dogs' lives may parallel his and Anne's if they do marry. His failure to infer meaning from the Pekes does not mean that readers are unlikely to do so. In effect, Mansfield allows readers to make any number of possible comparisons by not causing her narrating consciousness to make one of its own. Things are different with the doves. Here Anne supplies the comparison: A man obsequiously following around after a woman who laughs at him may be "all very well for Mr. and Mrs. Dove. But imagine that in real life—imagine it!" she commands of Reggie and of the reader. But we readers must ask whether Mansfield means for us to accept as completely accurate Anne's interpretation of the doves. Just because Anne sees her possible marriage as resembling the doves' does not mean that it will be that way.

The characterization of Anne and Reggie, however, seems to support the view that he will follow her around and give in to her demands and that she will laugh at him throughout their lives together. If such be the reading, then Reggie is weak and Anne is nasty. She seems almost to have manipulated Reggie into the marriage that the conclusion of the story forecasts. But since he obviously wants to marry her from the beginning, why does she not simply accept him in the first place? What is her point in putting him through all this torture, sending him away only to call him back? Does she honestly not know her own mind? Or is she really the cat staying just far enough away from the mouse to make the game interesting? Or does she feel a need to prove to herself that she can control him? Might she be trying to get him to stand up to her but, seeing that such will never be the case, calls him back in order to torment him further, simply to exercise her superiority over him? The story provides no evidence that Anne lacks other marriage possibilities or is dangerously close to going beyond the marriageable age. Reggie seems to be a relatively simple character in contrast to Anne, who may be playing games or roles. In fact, Anne is one of the more complex female characters, perhaps as complex as Mansfield herself. In any case, Anne inhabits a challenging story, one in which the two other pairs of naturally mated "animals" must somehow be interpreted as making a contribution to every reader's version of whatever "kind of truth" Mansfield does achieve in the story.

"Mr. and Mrs. Dove" and "The Stranger," along with a 1914 story entitled "Something Childish but Very Natural," all illustrate the strong tendency of Mansfield's stories to portray women with much more complicated psyches or personalities than the male characters have. Admittedly, this characterization does not set Mansfield apart from the majority of fiction writers or, for that matter, from a reality in which females are apparently the more complex of the sexes, especially regarding emotions, or at least the ability and willingness to use and display emotions that men traditionally sublimate, refuse to use, or cannot use. What is particularly interesting, however, about Mansfield's three stories is that the male seems to be set up to elicit at least equal sympathy in "The Stranger" and to deserve the greater sympathy from readers (of both sexes) in both "Mr. and Mrs. Dove" and "Something Childish." Another qualifying observation about the male characters in these last two stories is that unlike Mr. Hammond in "The Stranger," neither one is portrayed as being conventionally masculine.

"Something Childish" depicts the young love between an almost eighteen-year-old Henry and a barely sixteen-year-old Edna, who first meet on a train departing from London one Friday evening. Told again through the indirect male perspective, this story pictures Henry as a relatively simple, infatuated, innocent youth who pursues Edna by returning to that train, on Monday evening, hoping to meet her again. The reader is privy to all Henry's feelings of love and torment but has no way of knowing whether Edna at this time has any interest in seeing Henry again. Their first meeting has yielded no information about Edna's attitude toward Henry.

At that first meeting the only significant thing Edna says is that Henry's hat has left a mark on his head, a comment that becomes significant not at face value but because Henry is "madly excited" by it. Henry is for some reason almost beside himself over this simple statement, characterizing Edna's words as "marvellous" and as "in some mysterious fashion" establishing "a bond between them" (*KM*, 168). Perhaps anything she could say about him at this time would have triggered Henry's enthusiastic response. What she actually says must be taken as being of much less value than how Henry responds to it. He also characterizes the words as simple and natural, perhaps causing some readers to wonder whether Mansfield means to produce a connection between "simple and natural" and the words *childish* and *natural* of the title. If so, then the connection between Henry's hearing the words as mysterious and most readers' ideas of childishness and naturalness becomes interesting. Why should it be at all mysterious for a sixteen-year-old girl to say natural and childish things? Surely what she has said is well within any range of expectations. Therefore, Henry must be reading too much into her statement. Although he can characterize it accurately as simple and natural, his strong needs—perhaps for someone to take any kind of interest in him—excite him beyond what those words might be expected to do for most persons in a similar context. Mansfield illustrates how words can simultaneously have a general, simple, natural meaning while taking on an idiosyncratic meaning for a given listener.

Not surprisingly, Henry, excited about the girl and her simple words, stays in an emotional turmoil until they meet for a second time, on the train on Monday evening. This time they exchange names, and in the narrative passages surrounding that action Mansfield writes that both are "trying not to tremble so" and that after finding out each other's names they are "a shade less frightened" (*KM*, 169). After they tell their ages, Mansfield writes that "they looked at each other with a sort of desperate calmness. If only their bodies would not tremble so stupidly!" (*KM*, 170).

In a story that has previously been told entirely but indirectly through Henry's consciousness, these quoted phrases are either his view of the two of them or objective facts supplied by the narrator; in their wording, the statements read like objective facts. Nevertheless, it is difficult to interpret Mansfield's handling of this scene. Nowhere in the story does Mansfield directly write about Edna's consciousness. We know only what Edna says aloud, never anything that she thinks or feels, except for what she says in one letter that she writes to Henry. Her external actions are almost always those seen by Henry, as if reflected in his eyes. These quoted lines, however, seem to convey an objective report of what Edna is feeling in unison with Henry.

A simple (perhaps too simple) New Criticism explanation is that Mansfield has violated her own imposed point of view. For example, after Henry and Edna exchange names, the narrative reads, "in the pause they took possession of each other's names and turned them over and put them away, a shade less frightened after that" (*KM*, 169). The sentence is about what is going on in both minds. It seems to be a very clear sentence. But is it? Or does the sentence say exactly what it says yet not mean what it says? In this story three such sentences all come in the immediate vicinity of the couple's exchanging of names and ages. Because nowhere else in the story does Mansfield do anything similar, it is hard to believe that she allowed the same "blemish" on her story to appear three times. No, something has happened to Henry's perspective, not to Mansfield's craft. Henry so fully projects his feelings onto Edna that Mansfield feels no need to tell the reader what he is doing. In a narrative told completely through his indirect consciousness, his distortion of Edna's emotions to fit his own cannot be explained directly by Mansfield; her doing so would have created a real blemish on the story. Henry's earlier emotional enhancement of Edna's mentioning the hat mark on his head should help prepare the reader for this shift of his emotions onto her psyche. Although a sentence similar to these three appears later, when the narrative reads, "They did not want to go home," that narrative sentence is soon followed by Edna's saying, "Oh dear, I don't want to go home" (*KM*, 177). The other three sentences are not accompanied by any dialogue or descriptions of Edna's physical actions that manifest the feelings she is said to harbor.

This passage probably causes many readers to feel that Henry and Edna are indeed soul mates, made for each other, exceedingly compatible in their feelings. As the story continues, however, most readers surely realize that the emotions flow primarily in one direction, from Henry to Edna. What Henry sees and hears bouncing back off her resembles more nearly what he desires than what actually exists.

Perhaps only Henry is childish and natural. As he and Edna are talking about their occupations and activities and how they hate their ordinary jobs, she suddenly says, "My mother is a Hungarian—I believe that makes me hate it even more." Thinking that this cause and effect is "quite natural," Henry responds, "It would." Edna goes on to say that she and her mother are "exactly alike" but that she has nothing in common with her father, who is "just . . . a little man in the City" (*KM*, 171) (perhaps like Henry?). And she declares that she has her mother's wild blood, a statement made in the face of words and actions that belie such a thing. Edna cannot stand, for example, for Henry to touch her. Henry keeps declaring that they are naturally drawn to each other and know all about each other. Mansfield is clearly demonstrating that Henry is being very natural and very childish, especially when he says "very solemnly: 'I believe we're the only two people alive who think as we do'" (*KM*, 172). It is natural for him to believe such a thing at his age, in love apparently for the first time.

Edna is more complex, though younger. At a concert the following weekend, she seems selfish and pushy, demanding that Henry give her the program and refusing to look at it with him. She continues to refuse to let him hold her hand. After the concert she suddenly declares that she is not going to take the train with him. After many tears, pleadings, and recriminations, she tells Henry that she does not know why she refuses to let him hold her hand or kiss her, but after struggling aloud with her reasons and emotions, she declares that if they kissed they would not "be children any more . . . silly, isn't it"? (*KM*, 175). She pleads for Henry's understanding of her fears but receives only a weak "Yes, I think I do." Whether Henry understands her or not, the mature reader is surely supposed to be able to comprehend and sympathize with this natural and childish fear of growing up, of losing innocence, while at the same time being able to recognize the inevitability of its happening, for most persons. The reader cannot know at this point if it will happen to Edna.

The story moves to a general summary of Henry and Edna's next several weekends together, as "London became their playground" (*KM*, 175). They see houses and imagine themselves living in them. Although both take part in this game, Henry is by far the major player. He talks at length about how wonderful their life is, but Edna responds with short, agreeable, and agreeing statements. Something peculiar happens, however, when a kitten—real, not imagined—comes on the scene, goes to Edna, and is picked up and stroked by her. Henry continues to pretend, telling Edna to put the cat inside their house so that they may go for a walk and even pretending to open the door for her to do that. But he suddenly interrupts his pretending about the door and says, "Let's go away at once. It's going to turn into a dream" (*KM*, 177). That may seem like a strange attitude in a person who has been imagining their life together so vividly as to be able to know the name of their maid. Henry can live in his imagination more readily than he can handle pretending to let a real cat through a nonexistent door.

The episode makes Henry talk about not wanting to wait to have a real life together, to which Edna raises practical questions about their lack of money. She does not respond to his effort to get her to agree that "money is more or less accidental" and is "either there or it doesn't matter" (*KM*, 177). Instead, she looks "up at the sky" and says she does not want to go home—that is, to her real home, not the imaginary house she and Henry have been inhabiting. The honest pain of their relationship and unfulfilled yearnings come through in the story; Mansfield is not making fun of young love. Henry and Edna's love is childish in some ways but truly natural. Neither one seems to be playing any kind of romantic game with the other, as Anne may well be doing with Reggie in "Mr. and Mrs. Dove." Edna's reluctance to let Henry touch her stems not from designs to make him desire her even more ardently but from her natural fears about sensuality. She may say that she has the wild blood of her Hungarian mother, but she certainly does not allow that heritage to control her; the story gives no evidence that Edna's fears are based on social or moral lessons imbided from her environment.

The ensuing idyllic interlude in the woods sounds remarkably as if it might be a passage from D. H. Lawrence's *Sons and Lovers,* which Mansfield had read, at least in part, in the summer of 1913, prior to writing this story in Paris in December 1913 (Alpers, 160). The characters Paul Morel and Miriam Leivers in the Lawrence novel are, in fact, nineteen and sixteen, during the most intense portion of their relationship, detailed in the chapter entitled "Lad and Girl Love." Miriam and Edna share a fear of physical contact with the lover, and both make flowers a substitute outlet for their sensuality. Lawrence says that to Miriam "flowers appealed with such strength she felt she must make them part of herself."[13] Mansfield describes how Edna wades "into the heather" and lies down in it. Henry takes "some primroses out of her basket" and makes "a long chain to go around her throat." The confused feelings that Mansfield's young lovers have about themselves and their relationship are a great deal less extreme than those of Paul and Miriam, but in this one scene in the woods, Mansfield has created actions and emotions that resemble those created earlier by Lawrence. It should not be surprising that Mansfield at this time—less than a year after first meeting Lawrence and his wife Frieda—should have come creatively under the Laurentian spell; after all, he powerfully affected almost everyone he met.

Yet Mansfield certainly did not fall so far under Lawrence's spell as to approach his explicitness in describing sexual matters. Undoubtedly "Something Childish" reflects greatly the Murry-Mansfield love relationship at the time and the couple's long-running dream of having a home of their own, but it also speaks of the more universal "childish and natural" emotions that many young couples suffer through and that Mansfield could see in Lawrence and Frieda and in Jack and herself.

Perhaps, having seen in *Sons and Lovers* the tumultuous, extreme emotions of Lawrence and Frieda, Mansfield depicted in her story something that might almost be called a more normal, less extreme version of an age-old story of young love. She may also have viewed her and Jack's love as being like the Lawrences' but less psychically disturbing. Certainly the scene in the woods in Mansfield's story is emotionally toned down from any that Lawrence created. Although the word *idyllic* can be applied to Mansfield's story, probably no one has ever used that term to describe the Paul-Miriam relationship in *Sons and Lovers*.

One other point concerning Mansfield herself and this particular story is that she seems to have put more of herself into Henry than into Edna. Katherine Mansfield was more the aggressor in the early days of her relationship with Murry, inviting him first to live in her flat and then to become her lover. He seems to have been the one less inclined to move their friendship onto the physical plane.

Although "Something Childish" was Mansfield's longest story to date and the most emotionally complex, it was not published in a periodical or collected in book form until after her death, when it appeared in *Colliers* in 1924 and became the title story of her posthumous collection *Something Childish and Other Stories*. No specific evidence exists as to why Mansfield chose not to include it in the collections she put together; thus, we can only assume that she found her first major blending of reality and fantasy to be less successful than some of her later works in that vein.

Perhaps the inconclusive ending bothered Mansfield, but how else can the story end? Coleridge's poem of the same title as the story ends with the speaker dreaming that like a "little feathery bird" he can fly to his love, and Henry dreams at the end of "Something Childish" that Edna is coming to join him at their dream house. Fantasy, or dream, replaces fantasy, however, so that by the end nothing that can be remotely called reality exists in the story. Henry believes that he sees a "big white moth flying down the road" toward him, but it turns out to be a "little girl in a pinafore" who gives him a telegram, which may be "only a make-believe one, and it's got one of those snakes inside it that fly up at you" (*KM*, 182), Henry says to himself. In this dream, which is surely supposed to duplicate what the reader knows is the reality of the situation (that Edna is not going to join Henry), the telegram becomes "just a folded paper" and the garden becomes "full of shadows" that "span a web of darkness over the cottage and the trees and Henry and the telegram" (*KM*, 183). The closing sentence says that Henry does not move. The Keatsian mood is clearly evident: For Henry, was this whole affair "a vision, or a waking dream?" Does he "wake or sleep"? Both Mansfield's direct use of the Coleridge poem and her suggestion of Keats's "Ode to a Nightingale" push this story out of the realm of reality, where many of the specific details of the Henry-Edna courtship seem to place it, into a fantasy world in which a reader may well wonder whether Henry has not imagined the whole thing as the result of seeing a pretty girl on the train, with a "leather case on her lap with the initials E. M. on it."

As Henry looks at Edna with the Coleridge poem persisting "in his brain" and wonders whether she goes to school or works in an office, he seems to become entranced by her "beautiful waving hair" to the point of saying a line of poetry. The line reads, "My eyes are like two drunken bees . . ." and is followed by Henry's question to himself, "Now, I wonder if I read that or made it up" (*KM*, 166). The reader who at that point does not look back at the Coleridge poem printed in the story probably assumes that the line comes from the poem. But it does not. Henry has made it up, just as he has made up in his imagination everything that seems to occur within the story between himself and Edna after this point. The rest of the story reads as if it all really takes place (except when Henry and Edna do some "actual" imagining), until Mansfield gives us an obvious fantasy with the telegram business at the end, seeming to imply that such an imaginative experience as Henry's must feed on itself, growing so terribly real for him (and for the reader) that it can come to an end only by turning into a fantasy. Whatever else this compelling story may do for or to readers, surely it can pique the memories of many who as children very naturally lived in our own imaginative worlds.

Yet "Something Childish" is also a story about the pain that can come to a young person, almost an adult, who lives too long or too thoroughly in a world of fantasy and whose yearning for a reciprocated love and a permanent home resembles Mansfield's own in many respects. If she gave some of her more harsh traits to Janey of "The Stranger" and to Anne of "Mr. and Mrs. Dove," Mansfield provided one of her softer traits to Henry of "Something Childish but Very Natural."

The Lonely Characters

Katherine Mansfield also wrote several stories about lonely people whose lives are hard or who are emotionally or physically deprived. Not surprisingly, most of these stories are about older characters. Two of the ten stories that can be placed in this thematic group are among her best: "Miss Brill" and "The Daughters of the Late Colonel." The others range from a trio of impressionistic sketches of lonely women, lumped under the title "Spring Pictures," to a pair of stories—"Life of Ma Parker" and "The Woman at the Store"—much more in the naturalistic mode than is the bulk of Mansfield's work. Three of the ten have male protagonists: "An Ideal Family," "The Fly," and "Ole Underwood." The final two stories are "The Wrong House," actually a sketch in which undertakers come to the wrong house, almost frightening an old woman into needing their services, and "Pictures," a nearly maudlin treatment of a very old plot, that of the aging actress who goes from agency to agency in a vain search for a part in a play, only to give it all up and accept a bad offer from life itself, this time in the guise of a "stout gentleman" who blows "cigar smoke full in her face" and extends his invitation to her most bluntly: "Well, am I goin' your way, or are you comin' mine?" (*KM*, 401).

Questioning the fine line between sanity and insanity is one of Mansfield's apparent purposes in several of these stories, but there is little question that she depicts Ole Underwood as having crossed over that line. In New Zealand thirty years ago, this former sailor killed his wife because she was unfaithful to him while he was at sea. Having spent twenty years in prison for the crime, he is now a daily victim of his town's hatred and wrath. Called an "ole swine," he is banged over the head "with a tin jug" (*KM*, 136) and kicked out of the pub; a woman sloshes "a pail of slops over his feet" (*KM*, 137). All the time Ole's heart is depicted as banging in his chest with words that relate to his current activity or feelings: "Red—Red—Red!" (*KM*, 136) as he stares at flowers in the pub or "Kit! Kit! Kit!" (*KM*, 137) as a kitten rubs on his sleeve and reminds him of the kitten he once brought to his wife from his ship. Apparently this memory triggers deep emotions

58

and other recollections, because he vows to himself to do something—
"I will! I will! I will!" (*KM*, 137). The reader cannot know at this point
that Ole will seek revenge on his wife's seducer, a person not actually
known to Ole. Ole's lack of knowledge has been reported as apparent
fact by a man in the pub. Having thrown the kitten by its tail "out to
the sewer opening" (*KM*, 138) and feeling like a young man again, Ole
heads for a ship, which his heart (or crazed mind) tells him is "his
ship!" and then immediately shouts, "Mine! Mine! Mine!" (*KM*, 138).
Ole makes his way to a stateroom, where a man is described as sleeping
beneath a picture of Ole's long-dead wife. In Ole's mind this is his
own stateroom from thirty years ago; the picture of his wife is imagined
as being on the wall over the sleeping man. The implication in this
minor story is that Ole Underwood will kill this "big sleeping man,"
the latter becoming an innocent victim of a diseased, revengeful mind.
Ole's mind has placed what he takes to be his enemy in Ole's own
bunk, indicating a rational thought within the crazy whole.

In writing "An Ideal Family" some six months before writing "The
Fly" in February 1922, Mansfield seems almost to have been trying to
create the later, better, and far more famous story in her first effort.
Mr. Neave, the father of "An Ideal Family" of three daughters and
one son, looks like a composite of old Mr. Woodifield and the boss in
"The Fly." Because the two stories have so many similarities in both
form and content, it is reasonable to consider what "truth" Mansfield
may have been pursuing. She did say that in "An Ideal Family" she
"didn't get the deepest truth out of the idea, even once." She called
the "truth" of the story a "kind of knowledge" that was too easy for
her to achieve, "even a kind of trickery" (*Journal*, 257). Did she get
that truth in "The Fly" by adding the concept of the boss to the basic
formula of a weary old man much at the mercy of his wife and
daughters?

Both "old Mr. Neave," who feels "too old for the spring" (*KM*, 505),
and "old Mr. Woodifield," whose hands tremble when he tries to remember what he wants to tell the boss, feel themselves to be the victims of overprotective females. In "An Ideal Family" Mr. Neave, who
still goes to the office, where he is the boss, is continually accused by
his family of being unreasonable for doing so and is constantly ha-
rangued to retire, "take up some hobby," and "be happy" in staying
home in their "huge house and garden" "for a change" (*KM*, 507). In
"The Fly" Mr. Woodifield, who is already retired but apparently has
no hobby, is "boxed up in the house every day of the week except

Tuesday," when his family gets him dressed up and lets him "cut back to the City for the day. Though what he did there the wife and girls couldn't imagine" (*KM*, 597). With respect to the essential relationship between the male character and the female members of his family, both stories are much the same, although Mansfield provides a great deal more information about life at the Neaves' than she does about that at the Woodifields'. The reason for doing so, however, is necessitated by her placing the primary scene of "An Ideal Family" at home, whereas that of "The Fly" is in the office of the boss. Mr. Neave is in his office, however, when the story opens.

Although there are (or were) sons in both the Neave and the Woodifield families, what Mansfield does about those sons makes a crucial difference in the two stories. Mr. Neave's son, Harold, is alive, working in the business, but not greatly trusted by his father to take over and do things as they should be done. Mr. Neave remembers Harold's stealing some money from his mother's purse when he was thirteen and being too easily forgiven because "his mother, his sisters, and the servants" worship Harold and forgive "him everything." These thoughts on his way home from the office cause Mr. Neave to strike "sharply with his stick upon the pavement edge" (*KM*, 506) and to brood further about Harold and the business in a way that is the direct opposite of what the boss in "The Fly" thinks about his dead son.

The boss remembers his son as not "in the least spoilt" (*KM*, 600), in contrast with Mr. Neave's believing that everyone is helping to spoil Harold. The boss believes that his son was fully ready to take over the business before he was killed, but Mr. Neave knows that his son is not putting "his whole heart and soul into" (*KM*, 506) the business. Pointedly, Mr. Neave and Harold do not come home together; the boss and his son went into work and came home together daily.

In "The Fly" the sons of both Mr. Woodifield and the boss are dead, having been killed in World War I and buried close together in the same cemetery in Belgium. Mansfield provides no information about Reggie Woodifield's personality or relationship with his father while alive; Mr. Woodifield now speaks only about how "beautifully looked after" the cemetery is with "flowers growing on all the graves" (*KM*, 599). The boss, in contrast, does think about how his son (unnamed in the story) was while alive.

Most critics of the much-analyzed "The Fly" never raise the question that the boss in this memory of his son may be seriously distorting the way things really were, that the boy was more like Harold Neave as seen by his father: lazy, dishonest, conceited, forgiven too much by his mother and sisters—in short, worshiped as the only son and heir. "An Ideal Family" in its telling offers no reason to doubt the objective accuracy of Mr. Neave's view of his son; in contrast, "The Fly" offers several reasons to question the view that the boss has of his son.

Both stories conclude with their protagonists alone in a room, feeling wretched about their lives, their feelings displayed in similarly symbolic terms. Before being forced by his family to dress for dinner one more time, Mr. Neave has half-dozed in his chair, imagining "a little withered ancient man climbing up endless flights of stairs" (*KM*, 510). Now that he has been dressed by his young manservant, Charles, Mr. Neave again falls half-asleep in his bedroom and sees "that little ancient fellow" again, now "climbing down endless flights that led to a glittering, gay dining-room. What legs he had! They were like a spider's—thin, withered" (*KM*, 511). The actual fly that the boss torments into and out of the ink as a replacement for his own wretched state has been substituted in the later story for Mr. Neave's imagined spider.

In either case, Mansfield says both men feel that their lives have had no more meaning than bugs going up and down stairs or climbing into and out of puddles of ink. Whatever "truth" Mansfield is after in these two stories seems closely connected with her need to understand her own feelings about her dead brother Chummie and so grasp what her career had come to in 1921–1922, after having taken a new course as the result of Chummie's death. Mansfield may have placed herself into the roles of the boss and Mr. Neave. In worrying about the question of what a lifetime of work amounts to, Mansfield may very well have had the possibility of her own short career in mind, a career that would end with her death less than a year after she completed writing "The Fly."

Like so many of Mansfield's other stories, these two involve characters who are searching for the meaning of their lives or are being miserable because they think their lives lack meaning. Often such stories, largely because they contain sympathetic characters like Mr. Neave, appear to set forth some particular meaning of life. Both the boss and Mr. Neave have lived their only lives in their businesses so that they can pass those businesses on to their sons; establishing and maintaining a family business is what life is all about to them. But now Mr. Neave does not trust Harold with the business, and the boss's son is dead. Consequently, life has no meaning for these men, a situation they demonstrate with the spider-and-fly imagery. In his despair Mr. Neave thinks that life has passed him by and that the present woman, Charlotte, is not really his wife; his real wife is "that little pale girl" he married, and "all the rest of his life had been a dream" (*KM*, 511).

Perhaps the reason Mansfield said that she did not "get the deepest truth out of the idea" of "An Ideal Family" was that she knew she had allowed her story to make a convincing statement that a life like Mr. Neave's does lack meaning. Because he is such a sympathetic character, especially in contrast with his family members, and has reached an age when people are expected to start having a little wisdom to pass on, the reader is likely to take as truth his view about what life means or ought to mean. Mansfield knew, despite her own relentless searching and that of her characters, that the deepest (but most painful) truth about life is that we cannot know its meaning in terms as specific as Mr. Neave uses. The boss, who is an extremely unsympathetic character, is a much better bearer of the deeper truth that there is no truth. Truth is no more going to grow out of wretchedness than it is out of elation, with Mansfield's story "Bliss" serving as a case in point. Perhaps the tremendous amount of critical attention paid to "The Fly" is owed in large part to the presence of such a deeper truth about the meaning of life that few readers are willing to accept any other reader's view of what the story means.

Mansfield could not help pursuing the meaning of life, knowing full well that she would never find it, because it can be found only if there is some a priori definition by which it is recognized when seen. Jake Barnes in Ernest Hemingway's *The Sun Also Rises* states that deep truth which Mansfield knew but had a hard time admitting she knew, as perhaps most human beings do. Barnes, having done a little philosophizing about how best to live life, pulls himself up short to say that he really does not care "what it was all about. All I wanted to know was how to live in it. Maybe if you found out how to live in it you learned from that what it was all about."[14]

Mansfield's most famous story, "The Garden Party," states that truth as profoundly as she could put it. Laura, having experienced as obvious an a priori definition of "life" as can be imagined (that life is a garden party), has gone downhill to experience something her family knows cannot really be life, not there among the poor, who do not want to make anything of their lives. The poor do not know how to live, only how to die, and so Laura's mother really has no fear in exposing her daughter to death among the poor; life among them (as in "The Doll's House") would be another matter. Laura has an important experience with one *kind* of life and with one death, but the death is a universal one and the life is not. When Laura returns home, she naturally tries to make a universal statement about life; however, she cannot complete the statement, because of the deep truth that she has just learned but will probably have to keep relearning throughout her life. She stammers to her brother, "Isn't life . . . isn't life," and Mansfield allows him to say in understanding, "Isn't it, darling?" (*KM*, 549).

Stories such as "The Garden Party" and "The Fly" are strong and effective because they make open-ended statements about the meaning of life. In contrast, "An Ideal Family" supplies a particular definition of life—which perhaps explains why Mansfield knew she had failed to "get the deepest truth out of the idea."

"The Woman at the Store" and "Life of Ma Parker" depict the lives of lonely, work-scarred women, one in the backcountry of New Zealand and the other probably in England. The New Zealand story grew out of a trip to the "backblocks" taken by Mansfield in 1907 (Alpers, 56–59). The story is narrated with objectivity by a woman, traveling with two men. A woman at a store alleges that she and her daughter have been abandoned by her husband, but at the end of the story the girl makes a drawing of "the woman shooting at a man with a rook rifle and then digging a hole to bury him in" (*KM*, 134). The narrator and one traveling companion, Jim, are so shocked by the revelation that they sit "till dawn with the drawing beside" (*KM*, 134) them, but the other man, Jo, is apparently having sexual relations with the woman that night. Despite its vivid picture of the lonely rugged life, this 1911 story ends pointlessly in regard to the apparent killing, because Jim and the narrator ride off, with Jo shouting to them, "I'll pick you up later" (*KM*, 134). The piece only sketches in the different reactions of the three visitors.

"Life of Ma Parker," first published in 1921, is a more harrowing story of a deprived woman, largely because the woman is portrayed more directly than the one in "The Woman at the Store." In fact, "Life of Ma Parker" may be too harrowing. In killing off Ma Parker's husband and seven of her thirteen children, consigning two daughters to prostitution and two sons to emigration, sending another son "to India with the army," marrying the youngest daughter off to "a good-for-nothing little waiter who died of ulcers" (KM, 487), and then killing Ma's only grandson, Lennie, Mansfield may have piled death-in-life a little heavily onto her main character, a cleaning woman for a literary gentleman. Lennie's funeral has just been held, and so the pain is fresh and, finally, more than even the brave Ma Parker can bear. She thinks about how strong she has been through it all: "She'd kept herself to herself, and never once had she been seen to cry. Never by a living soul" (*KM*, 489). But now she knows that she needs to cry.

Mansfield's psychology in the story is sound, and her indictment of a society that has taught someone like Ma Parker that she must not be seen crying is devastating. The old woman tries to think of a place where she can "keep herself to herself" and cry as long as she likes, but there is no place: "She couldn't go home; Ethel was there. It would frighten Ethel out of her life. She couldn't sit on a bench anywhere; people would come asking her questions. She couldn't possibly go back to the gentleman's flat; she had no right to cry in strangers' houses. If she sat on some steps a policeman would speak to her" (*KM*, 490). Although "Life of Ma Parker" is not one of Mansfield's best stories, it is one of her most passionate cries "against corruption," the phrase Mansfield said precisely expressed her feelings about what some of her stories were supposed to be.[15]

In "Miss Brill" the character of the title is clearly as lonely as Ma Parker, but her equally painful story is told quite differently, largely because Mansfield supplies no background to account for why Miss Brill's Sunday passes as it does in the Jardins Publiques. Although Miss Brill in the course of the day is forced to see herself in a different light, the work is clearly a sketch, as Mansfield herself called it in a letter to Richard Murry. She told her husband's brother that she chose "not only the length of every sentence, but even the sound of every sentence . . . the rise and fall of every paragraph to fit her, and to fit her on that day at that very moment" (*Letters*, 360–61).

If the sentences and paragraphs are different for different points of Miss Brill's experience, then the sketch is in some sense a moving picture, or at least a changing one. It is certainly true that the picture Miss Brill has of herself suffers a forced change in the course of the afternoon. Mansfield also said in her letter to Richard Murry that she had read the story aloud many times, "Trying to get it nearer and nearer to the expression of Miss Brill—until it fitted her." Mansfield is saying here that form carries this story, which is certainly the case. In fact, the story *is* so completely the language with which Miss Brill records her world of the outdoor Sunday concert that the "story" remains most difficult to discuss. The tendency is just to quote those finely written, brilliant sentences. But Miss Brill herself is not brilliant; Mansfield subtly conveys the woman's lack of understanding of the world she observes so closely. Some of Miss Brill's poor comprehension may be owed to her advanced but indeterminate age. Just because she categorizes a great many of the people at the concert as "old" does not mean that Miss Brill herself is not also well along in years. Two sentences, in fact, say a great deal about Miss Brill's age, condition, and lack of self-awareness: Of the people who sit every Sunday in the same area where she sits, she notices "something funny about nearly all of them. They were odd, silent, nearly all old, and from the way they stared they looked as though they'd just come from dark little rooms or even—even cupboards!" (*KM*, 551).

Although many readers by this almost midpoint of the story may have begun to look askance at Miss Brill herself, the full effect of her observation of the others does not come until she goes home, her day ruined by a young woman's saying that her fox fur looks like "a fried whiting" (*KM*, 553). Miss Brill is so hurt that she does not even stop at the baker's to get her usual "slice of honey-cake," which sometimes has an almond in it. Tenderly demonstrating in what small ways a person may make her own life ever so slightly pleasant, Mansfield writes that the almond was to Miss Brill "something that might very well not have been there." Today without a slice of cake, she climbs the stairs to "the little dark room—her room like a cupboard" (*KM*, 553). Mansfield's handling clearly shows that Miss Brill has never before seen herself as being one of those funny old people. When she returns her fur to its box and puts on the lid, she thinks she hears something crying. Miss Brill herself, like Ma Parker, never has the good cry she so much deserves.

One of Mansfield's most successful stories is "The Daughters of the Late Colonel." Since the content of the story is such that obviously the two spinster sisters can never escape from the emotional prison in which their father confined them, Mansfield created a form in which the mazelike treatment of time also deprives them of the ability to achieve the kind of escape that might seem possible in a strictly chronological narrative. Because time is no more under the control of the sisters than are their wills, the story involves flashbacks and returns that are seemingly beyond their mental control, even when it is their thoughts that create the flashbacks. Even the reader has trouble keeping track of what day it is at any given point in a story that begins not at one point in time but with a whole week's worth of time, the week following some unnamed event.

The movement of "The Daughters of the Late Colonel" in time is not the only complication in form: The story is told from multiple points of view, moving from total omniscience through limited omniscience into the minds of the daughters. Distinguishing between words they actually say or merely think is difficult; the story goes without warning into their imaginations of the future and their memories of the past. These elements of a maze are complemented by a tone or attitude that has caused many a critic to comment on the bittersweet taste the story creates. Clare Hanson and Andrew Gurr say that reader response to the story requires an act of balancing between precisely matching shares of pathos and comedy.[16]

Mansfield acknowledged her own intentions in and attitudes toward the story in the areas of both form and content. She wrote to Richard Murry shortly after completing the "queer tale," telling him that in form it was both an outcome of the method used in *Prelude* and a new sort of thing, unfolding and opening out and being an advance on *Prelude* because "the technique is stronger" (*Letters*, 359). Following publication of the story, she commented on some receptions that seemed not to recognize her intentions. She told fellow fiction writer William Gerhardi that she had in her first conception seen the sisters as "amusing; but the moment I looked deep (let me be quite frank) I bowed down to the beauty that was hidden in their lives and to discover that was all my desire" (*Letters*, 388–89).

The story requires of the reader less of a balancing act than a willingness to enjoy a mental and eye game that can be simultaneously entrancing and discouraging, as the reader tries to discover a beauty in the lives of the sisters that is created by the beauty of Mansfield's form. If a maze can be both a pleasure and a challenge, so is Mansfield's story. It does, however, seem to reflect as well as any of Mansfield's stories the maze that each human weaves around herself, made up of the warp of nature and the woof of nurture. Some patterns of existence may seem more beautiful than others, but the taste says nothing about the essentiality of the pattern; once established, it must be completed or all the threads destroyed. Why this particular pattern of the Pinner sisters' lives developed is less important than its existence, which is not really affected by the father's death, even though the actions of the story are ostensibly all about the effects of that death.

The story opens at some point in time at least a week after the occurrence of some as-yet-undesignated event and then moves, in the second sentence, into a generalization about how at least two unnamed and unidentified persons went to bed each night during that week with their minds not going immediately to sleep but instead continuing to think, worry, and wonder about their maze. The general sentence about the nightly activities breaks off with an ellipsis that conducts the reader into the events of one particular night, which is clearly supposed to be representative of what happened every night during the week. Section 1 of this twelve-section story does not define the precise night on which this particular conversation takes place, although twice the sisters talk about doing something "to-morrow," which may or may not be within the week that, according to the first sentence of the story, is now finished. Indefinite time is matched by even more indefinite decisions made by Josephine and Constantia, daughters of the late Colonel Pinner. They reveal themselves here, as throughout the story, to be silly and pathetic, understandable and understanding, sympathetic, ineffectual, indecisive women, who have been effectively enslaved by their father.

If their father is dead, Nurse Andrews is very much alive and a serious problem for the sisters, because they have asked her to stay on a week as their guest and now they do not know how to get rid of her. This complication in their lives begins not because they are so generous but because they do not know how to tell Nurse Andrews that it is time for her to go. Although the sisters do not acknowledge any such feeling, they may have asked the nurse to stay as a connection to their dead father. So they delay. This complication in their lives is first stated as a generalization in Section 2 and then becomes (as in Section 1) a particular event, as a meal demonstrates with precise evidence the general problem the sisters have coping. Their young cook, Kate, is also introduced in this section, in a sentence that shows Mansfield's brilliance in handling the narration of this story: "And proud young Kate, the enchanted princess, came in to see what the old tabbies wanted now" (*KM*, 466). This melange of subjective attitudes and objective facts works well. "Young" is an objective fact, though relative, of course. The pride is in Kate, as is the characterization of the sisters as tabbies. But surely Kate does not think of herself as an enchanted princess, nor do the sisters probably ever call her that; however, they do treat her as if she were such a person, hesitating to disturb her to wait on them. The statement must certainly not be read as representing the attitude of a narrator; it is a statement to be taken as true, inasmuch as the sisters do act like tabbies and Kate surely must sometimes call them that behind their backs. The force of the sentence comes from a living three-part source (Kate, the sisters, and their relationship within the household) and one dead source: Colonel Pinner. The narrative voice is no more than a reporter of this sentence, not a creator of it. That narrative voice is separate from all the others but does not seem to judge or control anything but itself, making a more obvious reportorial statement from time to time. Such a statement closes Section 2 when Nurse Andrews's laugh is described as "like a spoon tinkling against a medicine-glass" (*KM*, 467). Reporters can use metaphorical language, too.

Section 3 is, surely by design, the shortest of the twelve sections, because it is the only one describing the actual death of Colonel Pinner. This event creates the story, but it is one that his daughters must hurry past. As the colonel dies, Nurse Andrews insists on remaining beside his bed, holding his wrist. Naturally, Josephine and Constantia resent her presence but cannot possibly ask her to leave. The section is told as if within the dual mind of the two sisters, both of them thinking precisely the same thoughts, though Mansfield says that they arrive at all common positions individually. Although, as we see later in the story, the sisters do have their differences about which one should go first in doing something, they are always going to do the same thing and think the same way. In unison here they think, "Supposing father had wanted to say something—something private to them" (*KM*, 467).

Having sent the reader down this path of sympathy in the maze, Mansfield immediately puts up a dead end with her next sentences: "Not that he had. Oh, far from it!" The judgment conveyed here that the colonel on his deathbed had absolutely nothing to say to his daughters might be that of the narrator, were the narrator making such judgments. It seems far better to read this idea as coming from the dead man himself, not in some supernatural way from the grave but as his parting nonwords to his daughters: as his saying to them that he really despises their abject servitude, even if it was he who helped force it upon them; he can hardly be given full blame for the relationship he for years has had with them. The section concludes with a description of the colonel's last moment, when to his daughters' consternation he opens not both eyes but only one eye, making all the difference to their memory of him.

Mansfield effectively moves into the next section through a common pronoun, meaning that the reader has more help escaping the maze of form than the sisters have in escaping from the restricting maze of their lives. Section 3, speaking of the father's one open eye, reads, "It glared at them a moment and then . . . went out." Section 4 picks up that pronoun: "It had made it very awkward for them when Mr. Farolles, of St. John's, called the same afternoon" (*KM*, 467). To Mr. Farolles's opening words of assurance that "the end was quite peaceful, I trust," Josephine says, "Quite," but both hang their heads because they feel certain "that eye wasn't at all a peaceful eye" (*KM*, 468). Why should they be ashamed if their father has not died peacefully? Because they have given their lives to trying to satisfy him, to make him happy; obviously they have not succeeded, probably because they could not succeed with that man no matter what they had done. A strong implication of the glaring eye is that their father really despises them for taking care of his every need before satisfying any of their own. If they are seemingly his victims, he is equally in their thrall and cannot stand it that they are so much better than he. In a story that both Mansfield and LM knew to be in some ways about their own complex dependencies on each other, it is difficult to know which one is more like the dominating colonel and which one more like the truculent girls—probably Mansfield saw a little of both of the fictional antagonists in herself and LM. If the fictional version is an emotional maze, the real-life relationship was probably even more complex.[17]

As Mr. Farolles's innocent initial question upsets the daughters, so, too, does his equally innocent suggestion that they might want him to serve communion prove devastating to their emotions. In fact, Mansfield characterizes the idea as terrifying the sisters internally, but Josephine and Constantia fail to give oral expression to any of their several reasons for being terrified: in the drawing room, with no altar (the piano is too high); someone will interrupt; the doorbell might ring. All these unstated reasons are objections only to the form of the possible communion, not to the need for having such a service conducted. In causing her characters to feel nothing but objections to form, Mansfield implies that the real objection is to the content itself. The sisters do not want—cannot religiously or psychologically tolerate having—a communion at this time with the terrifying thought that they will be drinking and eating not of Christ's but of their father's body and blood. How can they possibly celebrate a mass for a man who in his life sucked all the lifeblood out of them? This is a fact that deep in their souls they know but can never allow to rise to the surface. The symbolic values of communion at this time would for them be totally removed from the religious into the personal and psychological. Thus, the only thing that Mr. Farolles can do for them is to promise to send the undertaker, Mr. Knight (whose name produces ironic values in both spellings), to see them in the belief that they "will find him very helpful indeed." The priest has not been much help. Perhaps Mansfield means that priests and religion cannot really provide escapes from the kind of emotional maze in which the sisters have lived most of their lives.

Apparently Mr. Knight is helpful, because Section 5 begins with the funeral arrangements and the burial all behind them: "Well, at any rate, all that part of it was over, though neither of them could possibly believe that father was never coming back" (*KM*, 469). This section then goes into a flashback to the cemetery, where Josephine again reveals how close to the edge of insanity they have been driven. She fears her father's reaction when he finds out they have had him buried without his permission, but even more she fears his reaction to the bill: "And do you expect me to pay for this gimcrack excursion of yours?" (*KM*, 469), she imagines him saying. Both the humor of this reaction and the sisters' "normal" feeling that the money is always father's, even when it is actually going to be theirs now, should keep a reader from believing that Josephine and Constantia really are insane. All their reactions to their father and his death are based too much on the reality of the situation for them to be seen as beyond the edge of cause-and-effect sanity.

The sisters next discuss whether they should have kept their father's body at home, "just for a time at least." This desire is again a marvelous blending of the absurd and the sensible, as Mansfield has Constantia, or Con, say, "We couldn't have kept him unburied. At any rate, not in a flat that size" (*KM*, 470). At this point many readers may be reminded of Emily Grierson in William Faulkner's "A Rose for Emily," written some eight years after Mansfield's story. Thinking of Faulkner's sympathetic treatment of Miss Emily, who so desperately needs love that she can keep Homer Barron's decaying body in her bed and even lie beside it, we may be helped in achieving a reading of Mansfield's story that sees the Pinner sisters as remaining within the bounds of sanity. Neither Faulkner nor Mansfield has written a case study of abnormal psychology, but each has achieved a penetrating examination of some of the terrible pains we human beings can inflict upon one another and upon ourselves.

Section 5 ends with Josephine's asserting tearfully that "father will never forgive us for this—never" (*KM*, 470). And Section 6 opens with the same assertion but now a part of the sisters' dual thoughts, as "two mornings later" they enter his room "without knocking even" (*KM*, 470) and start to go through his things. Again, in their thinking that they should knock, the daughters illustrate the effects that habitual conduct has on any person's actions; Josephine and Con are not mentally disturbed in thinking about knocking but are instead the victims of their own habit. This crucial, pivotal, and longest section of the story continues to illustrate the grip the man, even in death, has on them and will have for the rest of their lives. Mansfield in this section for the first time illustrates that these two women are not psychologically and emotionally identical twins, a fact that might give a reader some hope of one or the other escaping from their yoked journey.

Arguing about which one should be first through the door into their father's room, Josephine, or Jug, pushes Con forward, but Con complains that she should not go first, because Jug is the older. Jug is almost ready to use her "very last weapon," the assertion "But you're tallest" (*KM*, 470), when Kate comes on the scene. Josephine pretends that the door is stiff. The story then reads, "As if anything ever deceived Kate!" (*KM*, 471). The previously discussed sentence, also involving Kate, when the daughters are thought of as tabbies, is much like this sentence about Kate's never being deceived. This later sentence should not be thought of as an arch comment tossed in by the narrator or the author. It again represents a fact that all three characters fully understand. In a story in which Mansfield plays fast and loose— and successfully—with many objectivist notions about consistent handling of angle of narration, this statement makes a great deal of sense. All three characters are aware that Kate is not being fooled, and all three think it (or just plain know it without thinking) simultaneously. If any one of them were to state this knowledge, the words would be expressive of that individual, and so the collective thought here must be expressed in words that are not anyone's in particular but do represent a general sense that could come from each one. The sentence works, regardless of what someone's preconceived rules may be.

Once in the room, the sisters waver before the chest of drawers, unable to open it. Constantia's suggestion that they not open anything, "not for a long time," is met by Josephine's saying that "it seems so weak" not to go on and do what needs to be done. Constantia argues that "for once in our lives" we should be weak, because "it's much nicer to be weak than to be strong" (*KM*, 472). Having been nice to her father and weak in the face of his demands for most of her life, she speaks the truth, but she also demonstrates what an amazing misunderstanding the sisters have of their own actions, thinking they have been strong all these years in keeping the household going for their father, believing that it is weak to do something for one's own sake. Having argued that they should be weak and not sort out their father's things just now, Con does "one of those amazingly bold things that she'd done about twice before in their lives; she marched over to the wardrobe, turned the key, and took it out of the lock" (*KM*, 472), leaving the reader wondering why this is a bold rather than a weak action. The sisters both understand it to be bold because Con had "risked deliberately father being in there among his overcoats" (*KM*, 472). Again, there is sense in this attitude. Their father's spirit lives with them and will do so "forever," in their minds. The story says that he is still the dominant force in their lives; it does not say that they are crazy to let it be so. The section ends with an unexplained flashback in Jug's mind, as she leaves the room, remembering how at some time past she had followed Con after the latter "had pushed Benny into the round pond" (*KM*, 472).

The way Mansfield introduces Josephine and Constantia's brother, Benny, implies that they have not previously thought about him; certainly he has not previously been mentioned in the story. Their not thinking about him out there in Ceylon would certainly seem appropriate to their selfless selfishness in seeing their father's welfare as entirely their own burden and obligation. When in the next section (7) Josephine says, "Speaking of Benny" (*KM*, 473), even though Benny has been only in her mind and not on her tongue, Constantia "immediately looked" as if he had been mentioned. They discuss first not what to send but the difficulties of getting anything to him because there is "no post. Only runners." At these words, both pause "to watch a black man in white linen drawers running through the pale fields for dear life, with a large brown-paper parcel in his hands" (*KM*, 473). Retaining her own kind of verisimilitude and humor in this dual imagination of one action, Mansfield writes that "Josephine's black man was tiny" (she is the shorter daughter) but Constantia's is a "tall, thin fellow." With an ellipsis at the end of what is clearly Con's imaginative picture of her black man, Mansfield probably means that the separate imaginative views are ended and the reader is returned to a common view in the sisters' minds of Benny standing on his veranda, "dressed all in white and wearing a cork helmet" (*KM*, 473).

Section 7 ends with a paragraph in which Mansfield playfully deals with both the emotions of these women and the element of time, the two major factors in the story. Con is aware of one piece of wordplay in what she says about the watch arriving at Benny's home in Ceylon but is not aware of the second: "'And of course it isn't as though it would be going—ticking I mean,' said Constantia, who was still thinking of the native love of jewelry. 'At least,' she added, 'it would be very strange if after all that time it was'" (*KM*, 474).

Using her section divisions to set the story off in new directions, perhaps finally out of the maze, Mansfield begins Section 8 with the statement that Josephine makes no reply to Con's statement about the watch; rather, she flies "off on one of her tangents" (*KM*, 474), suddenly thinking about Cyril, another new piece in the puzzle of their lives. Josephine thinks at length about how it would be "more usual" for their father's only grandson to have the watch. This thought takes her sensibly to thinking about how if Cyril has the watch they will be able to see it in the future, when he comes to tea, which causes her to think about Cyril's note saying he could not attend the funeral, which causes her to say, "It would have been such a point in having him" (*KM*, 474), which causes Con, "not thinking of what she was saying," to reply, "He would have enjoyed it so" (*KM*, 475). This train of thought and action is interrupted by another of those dual thoughts that almost reads as if the narrative voice is speaking: "However, as soon as he got back he was coming to tea with his aunties [Cyril's word in their thoughts]. Cyril to tea was one of their rare treats" (*KM*, 475). Immediately, dialogue begins in an actual scene of Cyril at tea, a scene the reader probably first assumes is taking place in the future in the imaginations of the sisters but turns out to be a memory of a tea with Cyril while the colonel was still alive. Another dead end and another beginning.

The most humorously absurd piece of business in the story takes place in Sections 8 and 9, as the sisters together remember this particular tea with Cyril. They ask him if his father (Benny) is "still fond of meringues." Cyril "breezily" responds that he does not "quite know," to which Josephine almost snaps, "Don't know a thing like that about your own father, Cyril?" (*KM*, 475). More than humor lies in this exchange; Mansfield again is implying how little of importance these two sisters had always known about their own father, even if they did know some of the things he liked to eat. The validity of this reading is demonstrated when the sisters finally get Cyril (in Section 9) into the colonel's room and take turns shouting at the deaf old man that Cyril's father is still fond of meringues. Pathetically and humorously, the sisters tell the colonel four times, finally getting through to him, at which point he looks Cyril "up and down" and says, understandably, "What an esstrordinary [*sic*] thing to come all this way here to tell me!" Mansfield writes simply, "And Cyril felt it *was*" (*KM*, 478). Obviously, the daughters have no such reaction, showing again how things that might seem extraordinary to most persons have become, through habituation, normal events and attitudes to them.

Section 10 begins when present reality and Kate the cook burst in on the daughters and take them (and the reader) all the way back to the beginning of Section 7, when they are sitting in the dining room, after leaving father's room untouched, wondering if they dare "ask Kate for two cups of hot water?" (*KM*, 473). Apparently they never screwed up their courage enough to ask her, for she bursts in on them, boldly demanding to know "fried or boiled?" (*KM*, 478). Of course, the sisters are bewildered; of course, they debate the relative virtues of fried and boiled fish, after Kate tells them what she means; of course, they defer to each other until Kate proclaims, "I shall fry it." This confrontation sends them scurrying to the drawing room,where they imagine getting rid of Kate and fantasize about how they can cook for themselves. The section ends with Jug saying that on the question of whether they really "do trust Kate or not," that "just on this one subject I've never been able to quite make up my mind?" (*KM*, 479). The reader by this time surely must have concluded that these sisters will never escape the maze, especially as in Section 11 they fruitlessly discuss previous attempts to trap Kate and conclude in Josephine's words that they cannot postpone a decision again, because "if we postpone it this time—" (*KM*, 480).

Of course, Josephine's sentence is unfinished because another path presents itself to them, when the sounds of a barrel organ reach them from the street. The old spontaneous reaction that hits them anew is to start to run for money to pay the organ-grinder to leave so that their father will not start thumping on the floor with his stick. They realize in this final section of the story that their father died a week ago today, a Saturday, and they forget "to be practical and sensible" (*KM*, 481) and instead become emotional. Constantia looks at her "favourite Buddha," who always gives her the queer feeling of a "pleasant pain," actually the feeling that Mansfield must have intended her readers to get from this story. They look at their mother's thirty-five-year-old picture and wonder if their lives would have been different had she lived: "Might they have married?" Remembering their prospects, they do not seem to think so. Constantia, still looking at the Buddha, seems to get a different message, though one she has experienced before; "her wonder was like longing," as she remembers times in the past when she had "crept out of bed in her nightgown when the moon was full and lain on the floor with her arms outstretched, as though she was crucified" (*KM*, 482). She credits "the big, pale moon" with having made her do it and remembers not minding when the "horrible dancing figures on the carved screen had leered at her." Continuing, Constantia recalls passionate moments "off by herself," "as close to the sea as she could" get, singing "something, something she had made up, while she gazed all over that restless water" (*KM*, 483).

Clearly, then, Con once had her own feelings and desires, had the chance to do something for herself, felt her sensuality. But there was "this other life"—taking care of father—that Con now sees as all having "happened in a kind of tunnel," from which she only occasionally escaped "into the moonlight or by the sea or into a thunderstorm," at which times "she really felt herself" (*KM*, 483). Passionate but silent questions before the Buddha about what it means, what "she was always wanting," lead at this too-late date only to the questioning words "Now? Now?" But "now" *is* too late, and so Con turns "away from the Buddha" (who knows what she does not know) and, "with one of her vague gestures," tries to say "something frightfully important" to Josephine, who interrupts Con's unfinished statement with an unfinished statement of her own. They defer to each other at such length that both say they have forgotten what they meant to say. Before Con started her long reverie about her few moments of almost escaping from the tunnel, the "thieving sun" had been out and had "touched Josephine gently," but now "a big cloud" sits "where the sun had been." And all possibility of their ever escaping the maze or the tunnel is gone forever, and they shall never live as anything other than what they have been all their lives, "The Daughters of the Late Colonel."

Stories of Young Girls

In addition to the heavily autobiographical Kezia stories, Mansfield wrote a number of other stories about girls and young ladies growing up. Two of these stories involve a shift from the Burnell family to the Sheridans, but the nature of the family is not greatly changed. Although the Laura Sheridan of "Her First Ball" and "The Garden Party" may not be simply an older Kezia Burnell, Laura does share with Kezia a sensitivity to the human condition that their sisters seem to lack. Two other stories about girls approaching womanhood do not involve well-to-do New Zealand families; they are "The Little Governess" and "The Young Girl." A fifth story discussed in this chapter remains one of Mansfield's most controversial stories. Her own father made one of the most damning critical comments on it when he threw *Je ne parle pas français* "behind the fire place" and said, "It wasn't even clever" (Alpers, 313).

It is worth noting that the husband-wife conflict is eliminated from "Her First Ball," a minor story, and barely hinted at in "The Garden Party," Mansfield's most anthologized piece of short fiction. A father does not appear at all in "Her First Ball" and is present only briefly in the other story, though long enough to perform telling actions. His daughter Laura begs him to let the band members "have something to drink." His failure to reply suggests that they are not allowed to. Offered a sandwich by Laura, he takes it and downs it in one bite, downs a second, and then tells his family about the "beastly accident" that is at the heart of the action in the story but that they have already heard about. Mrs. Sheridan considers his telling them "very tactless of father . . . " (*KM*, 545). Mansfield's ellipsis casts a shadow of indistinguishable shape over the couple's relationship.

"Her First Ball," written shortly before "The Garden Party," barely introduces the Sheridan family;—the sisters, Meg, Jose, and Laura, and their brother, Laurie. But it does establish the special relationship between Laura and Laurie that in "The Garden Party" will cause the latter to be the only one who understands Laura's feelings and sympathizes with her action of going to the dead man's home. The special relationship between Mansfield and her brother Chummie and that between Laura and Laurie Sheridan, coupled with the fact that the son is not yet a factor in the Burnell family but is a young adult in the Sheridan family, raises interesting questions about why, as the Burnells got older, Mansfield converted them to Sheridans. The Burnells' son is the youngest child in the family, but Laurie Sheridan is definitely older than Laura, although he may not be older than his other sisters.

As Leila, cousin of the Sheridans and the central "consciousness" of "Her First Ball," excitedly prepares for her first formal dance, she sees Laurie lean "forward and put his hand on Laura's knee," asking that she save two dances for him. Leila, much aware of being an only child, thinks "how marvellous to have a brother!" (*KM*, 512). Mansfield does an amazing job in the story of creating the twinkling words and dazzled thoughts of the eighteen-year-old Leila, who is thrilled to be entering into these exciting new activities. The experienced reader of Mansfield knows, of course, that there must be some leavening agent lying in wait for the much-too-happy Leila. This time it takes the form of "the fat man," who says he has been "doing this kind of thing for the last thirty years" (*KM*, 517), measuring out his life in dancing shoes, and providing his current partner with a most-Prufrockian "It hardly bears thinking about, does it?" To these words Leila most innocently says, "I think it's marvellous to be still going on." Of course, the man presses her a little too close but also tells her how, as a woman, she cannot possibly expect to be in the dancing crowd as long he has been: "Long before that you'll be sitting up there on the stage, looking on, in your nice black velvet. And these pretty arms will have turned into little short fat ones" (*KM*, 517). Such talk frightens Leila because it sounds so true. She asks herself a question, whose philosophical answer has to be yes: "Was this first ball only the beginning of her last ball after all?" (*KM*, 518).

Mansfield, as author, obviously knows the right answer to this question for both the existential philosopher and the eighteen-year-old girl, but she also knows and demonstrates that the continuation of the dancing lives of the Leilas of this world is at least as much a part of life as this poetic recognition: "In my beginning is my end."[18]

Leila pulls on her gloves and tries to smile; "deep inside her a little girl threw her pinafore over her head and sobbed. Why had he spoiled it all?" (*KM*, 518). Leila is, indeed, having her first real ball, crying for the first time in her life about her own mortality, acting out in fiction what Gerard Manley Hopkins called "the blight man was born for."[19]

It is herself she mourns for, but at this point she cannot really know that. She is only eighteen; thus, as soon as she begins dancing again, only "out of politeness," of course, she finds that "the lights, the azaleas, the dresses, the pink faces, the velvet chairs, all became one beautiful flying wheel" and when the fat man bumps into her, she smiles at him "more radiantly than ever. She didn't even recognize him again" (*KM*, 518). Most eighteen-year-olds do have, as Mansfield notes, that wonderful resiliency to bounce back, shrug off their own mortality, and go on dancing. For some solemn poets and philosophers, such a way of living is to be pitied and for others, scorned. But for Mansfield, it is to be depicted honestly and without sentimentality as one of the many facts of life.

As forced thoughts of her own inevitable death momentarily intrude on Leila's happiness in "Her First Ball," so, too, does a real death slightly upset the Sheridan family's garden party and result in the exposure of Laura Sheridan to death in such a highly dramatic and personal way that most readers leave "The Garden Party" believing that young Laura has been permanently affected and will not so easily be able to return to the dance of life. Her closing assertion or question, "Isn't life—" (which her brother, Laurie, understands), can be seen to resemble Hopkins's equally tantalizing words about how the young girl of his poem can come, in some mysterious way, to know that humans are born for death: "Nor mouth had, no nor mind, expressed/What heart heard of, ghost guessed" (Hopkins, ll. 12–13).

Laura's mind cannot create the words for her to say aloud what truths about life this experience has brought to her, but Mansfield suggests that some spiritual connection between brother and sister does exist. As a matter of fact, some spiritual connection exists between Mansfield and many of her readers: We call it "The Garden Party," a story whose message about human life and death is perfectly clear until we try to capture all that it says in a sentence or even a whole bundle of sentences. Although we readers may feel good that Laura is able to "suffer" such an emotional encounter, just as we may feel good that we are able aesthetically to enjoy her suffering, we should not believe that Mansfield is saying Laura has learned some lifelong and life-changing lesson, anymore than we can possibly believe that we have accomplished anything major for ourselves in "feeling" the story. If Laura and we readers have experienced something resembling a Joycean epiphany, that fact alone is good, but we must be aware of the impending antiepiphany or simply the mundane quotidian that will inevitably follow. Neither Joyce nor Mansfield in the short stories, however, does more than create the epiphanies. Only in his novels does Joyce have the scope to reveal the ordinary life that a Laura Sheridan, Gabriel Conroy, or John Hammond faces up to the next day. Mansfield, unfortunately, was not able to complete a novel.

"The Garden-Party" is a superior story to "Her First Ball," at least in part, because the development of Laura's inherent ability to be affected by the experience begins early in the story. Admittedly, Leila's experience with the fat man at the ball in no way emotionally resembles Laura's encounter with the death of the carter; however, if we can project Leila's character into "The Garden Party," we can see, I believe, that she would not have been capable of going down the hill to the other house. Leila's ability to shrug off the fat man's words is more like Jose Sheridan's ability to say to Laura "You won't bring a drunken workman back to life by being sentimental" (*KM*, 542) than it is like Laura's feeling that the garden party cannot go on. My contention is that the slightness of "Her First Ball" rests not just on the activity involved but also on the character taking part in it. Even if Mansfield had inserted a death into the ball, she could not have achieved what she attains in "The Garden Party" without major changes in Leila's character, to make her more nearly resemble Laura. Put another way, I am arguing that character, which reacts to and ultimately gives shape to the setting and meaning to the plot, is of greater significance than those other two factors, without which, of course, there may be no story. Leila and Laura define themselves through their actions, but what in them causes diverse actions remains the great mystery.

Laura Sheridan is apparently born with the same kind of inherent moral seismograph that Huckleberry Finn possesses. Whatever it is that causes Huck to help the slave Jim escape to freedom, thereby going against all the teachings of his religious, social, and political world, also causes Laura to want to stop the garden party upon news of the nearby death. Laura's similarity to Huck and her differences from her mother and sisters are developed from the beginning of the story, as Laura has "natural" reactions that go contrary to what her social and family environment says is right and proper. Laura's first reaction in the story is an environmentally induced guilty feeling that she should not appear before the workmen eating bread and butter, but she sets out to deal with them with the food naturally in her hand. Her first words to the workmen are "Good morning," in which she copies "her mother's voice. But that sounded so fearfully affected that she was ashamed" (*KM*, 535). Again, Laura's effort to use the "proper" voice in talking to workmen goes against something that she knows internally is right. One workman is not affected but has such an "easy" and "friendly" smile for Laura that she recovers her natural self. She knows from her social lessons that she "must be businesslike." When one of the workmen gives advice on where to erect a marquee, saying it should be put "somewhere where it'll give you a bang slap in the eye, if you follow me," Laura wonders because of her "upbringing" "whether it was quite respectful of a workman to talk to her of bangs slap in the eye. But she did quite follow him" (*KM*, 535).

Obviously, Laura has an easy, natural relationship with these men and is terribly uncomfortable trying to sustain the proper, inculcated one. This quality inherent in Laura's very being is established within the first two pages of the story and prepares the reader to accept as "right" her romantic and entirely impractical need (in her family's eyes) to do something about the dead man.

Mansfield, however, is as careful to keep Laura a believable human being, a mixture of the good and bad, as Mark Twain is to depict Huck, through Huck's own words, as a "real" fourteen-year-old. Huck can tell lies, when necessary, and rationalize his and Jim's need to steal food, and so Laura is pictured as going too far with her emotions in thinking that "she would get on much better" with a workman who takes a few seconds out to appreciate "the smell of lavender" than she does with the "silly boys" at the dances (*KM*, 536). Mansfield balances the account on Laura by causing her childishly "to take a big bite of her bread-and-butter" right in front of the workmen to demonstrate how she "despised stupid conventions" (*KM*, 536). When Laura gives her brother "a small, quick squeeze" and gasps, "Oh, I do love parties, don't you?" (*KM*, 537), she further demonstrates that she is still very young and very much a part of her society, whatever the nature of her built-in, sensitive moral seismograph.

Mansfield's point in developing, so successfully, a complex character in Laura is to show the contrast between the dogmatic self-righteousness and moral insularity of the comfortable rich and the open-minded girl on whom the facts of lives and deaths may still have some effect. As the author gives Laura a verisimilitude and a balance between being naive and understanding, so too, does she avoid piling sentimental notions on the heads of the poor carter's family down the hill. Their miserable physical existence does stand in stark contrast to the garden party of the Sheridans', but their confusion about life and death resembles Laura's. The widow of the dead man is described as not knowing why a strange girl is "standing in the kitchen with a basket," as wondering, "What was it all about?" (*KM*, 547). But if Mansfield cannot in honesty credit the poor with knowing what life is all about and will not make Laura utter a platitude about it after her experience, she does develop in Mrs. Sheridan a character who has all the wrong answers about it: "People of that class are so impressed by arum lilies" (*KM*, 546).

In this story Mansfield seems tacitly to forgive the poor because they are so busy just staying alive that they have no time to discover some other things that life can be; her censure is reserved for those who have apparently had money for such a short time that they have not even developed the sense of noblesse oblige that allegedly and traditionally accompanies the really rich. Mrs. Sheridan demonstrates her lack of it when she says to Laura, "People like that don't expect sacrifices from us" (*KM*, 543).

But what is to be done? Nothing. Like her fellow fiction writer Chekhov, Mansfield knew that nothing is to be done about the human condition through art except to show honestly how it is and maybe sometimes to cry out against the corruption. On her way down to the dead man's house, Laura stops a moment to think about how she is so filled up with the "kisses, voices, tinkling spoons, laughter, the smell of crushed grass" from the party that "she had no room for anything else" (*KM*, 546). Clearly, she does have room for a great deal more, even if she thinks she does not. Mansfield's best stories, such as "The Garden Party," create a condition in which we readers have the opportunity to make room for some things from the world around us other than those that occupy our daily lives. What we do with them, of course, is our own business.

"The Little Governess," written some six years earlier than "Her First Ball," also introduces a young lady to the unpleasant ways of men. Despite following the advice of "the lady at the Governess Bureau" to "mistrust people at first rather than trust them" (*KM*, 201), the young woman, who is heading to Germany to take a position with Frau Arnholdt, is nevertheless taken advantage of by three men: a porter in the railroad station, a waiter in her Munich hotel, and most seriously, a German whom she mistakenly thinks of for a short time as a protective grandfather and wonderful guide to things German. The two employees take revenge on her because she does not tip them properly.

None of these characters has a name. Most such stories would normally not contain names for porters and waiters, but Mansfield's omitting the names of the governess and her old "friend" seems to have significance—especially in the case of the man, who hands the girl his card, on which she reads only his title of privy councillor and decides that since he has a title, everything is "*bound* to be all right!" (*KM*, 210). Regarding the absence of the girl's name, perhaps Mansfield thought of governesses as a class of nameless souls. Most readers should know well before the little governess does that things are not all right, no matter what her new friend says. He tells her that German beer is not "at all like English beer," because it is not intoxicating, and so she drinks from "a glass like a flower vase" (*KM*, 211). She has to walk very close up against him under the umbrella to get out of the rain, but he forgets "to put down the umbrella" (*KM*, 211) when the rain stops. Having never seen "a bachelor's flat," she agrees to visit his, where he asks for "one little kiss before you go." She refuses, but he grabs her, holds her against the wall, and kisses her "on the mouth," where no one "who wasn't a near relation had ever kissed her before . . ." (*KM*, 213).

Fleeing back to the hotel where she is to meet Frau Arnholdt, the little governess discovers that her prospective employer has come and gone, with the waiter gaining his revenge by telling Frau Arnholdt that her potential governess has left with a man and that he has no idea when she will return. The story, to its detriment, also abandons the girl at the end, as Mansfield describes the emotions of the revengeful waiter. Mansfield seems to leave the girl there with no hints to the reader as to what her next step may be. Of course, the little governess may well have no idea what she is going to do, with little money in a strange country and her promised job apparently gone, but the reader should have received from the construction of the story some information on which to base a judgment about what happens next. In a story in which most readers are probably two or three steps ahead of the innocent girl in figuring out what is going to happen next, it seems unsporting of Mansfield to leave her readers in the same condition she leaves her little governess. No one learns anything from the experience.

A far better story is "The Young Girl." Here Mansfield returns to a first-person narration, but this is her only first-person story in which the sex of the narrator is not revealed. I have argued extensively elsewhere[20] that Mansfield, in order to keep any hint of sexual bias for or against her character's actions out of the story, must have consciously avoided using personal pronouns that would reveal the sex of the narrator. Nor could the title character of "The Young Girl" possibly reveal herself through the kind of internal dialogue that Mansfield uses to let Miss Brill, for example, discover something about herself. The seventeen-year-old daughter of Mrs. Raddick may be on the edge of self-discovery, but Mansfield knew not to push her over that edge. As evidence that she has passed beyond the childhood of her younger brother Hennie but is caught in that painful limbo between being a girl and being a woman, the narrator calls her Mrs. Raddick's daughter in the first sentence of the story. After that, she is referred to only with third-person-feminine pronouns, while her brother is regularly called by his name. For a narrator of either sex to call the girl by her given name or by Miss Raddick would possibly give away whatever relationship the narrator has with Mrs. Raddick that causes the narrator to be, in effect, baby-sitting.

Mrs. Raddick apparently dumps her daughter on the narrator so that she can gamble in a casino. Since the narrator has already agreed to entertain Hennie for the afternoon, one more person in the party does not seem like much trouble. Of course, the daughter is a great deal of trouble, as she pouts her way through tea, says she "really" does not want anything to drink, but then condescendingly says to the waitress, "Oh, you may as well bring me a chocolate, too." She uses her powder puff "as though she loathed it" and proclaims her cup of chocolate "dreadfully sweet!" (*KM*, 443). All in all, her actions are most obnoxious. She looks, however, as if she "might have just dropped from this radiant heaven" (*KM*, 440). Her horrid powder puff dabs a "lovely nose" and her "lovely eyes" look right through a "very good-looking elderly man" (*KM*, 444), who is obviously struck by her beauty. The little trio is supposed to return to meet Mrs. Raddick at an appointed time, but she is not there. And so when the narrator says, "I scarcely like to leave you" two here alone, the girl responds that she does not "mind it a bit. I—I like waiting." She blushes and almost cries, saying, "I love waiting! Really—really I do! I'm always waiting—in all kinds of places . . ." (*KM*, 445).

Indeed she is waiting, waiting for that magic and indiscernible moment when she will stop being a young girl and become a young woman. Until then, as Mansfield writes, she is "like a flower that is just emerging from its dark bud" (*KM*, 445). The narrator is not allowed by Mansfield to soften any description of how self-centered and obnoxious the girl really is, but at the same time, without ever saying so, that narrator provides a voice of quiet, understated sympathy and understanding. Maybe Mansfield thought that such objective reporting and subjective appreciation could not be convincingly portrayed in either a male or a female, which is why she so carefully removed sex as a factor in the narration. Whatever her motives in the story, Mansfield again has manipulated elements of form to shape the contents in a particular way.

Je ne parle pas français has been called Mansfield's "most complex and inaccessible" story (Hanson and Gurr, 66); it is certainly one of the most difficult to classify for purposes of discussion in relation to other stories. Because a young girl, abandoned by her lover, is of major concern in the story, it seems as reasonable to examine the story in this section as anywhere else. This vivid first-person narrative by a French pimp named Raoul Duquette involves a quite-simple story. Sitting in a bar, the extremely cynical Duquette, who alleges he really is a writer, confesses that he has had a moving experience. He has previously had an apparent homosexual relationship with an English writer named Dick Harmon, who has subsequently asked Duquette to take rooms in Paris for himself and a girl; the girl is named only Mouse. When Harmon and Mouse arrive in Paris, Duquette meets them and takes them to their rooms. Harmon excuses himself and goes to another room, ostensibly to write a letter to his mother. Instead, however, he writes a letter to Mouse and then disappears. The letter tells Mouse that her and Harmon's affair is finished because he cannot hurt his mother's feelings, "not even for you." Duquette, who insists in his confessional narration that he really did care for Mouse, promises her that he really will "look after you a little" (*KM*, 376). But he does not go back the next day, and he says that he "never saw Mouse again" (*KM*, 377). She is stranded in Paris with twenty pounds and no ability to speak French.

This story line, however, is not what makes *Je ne parle pas français* a fascinating and important story; the real significance lies in the narrator and his narration. Duquette has been seen as a Dostoevsky kind of character (Hanson and Gurr, 65). Mansfield, in a letter to Murry in February 1918, said that in reading a "fair copy" of the story, she "couldn't think where the devil I had got the bloody thing from—I can't even now. It's a mystery" (O'Sullivan, 2, 56). Although the story has been read by Murry and others as being highly autobiographical, with Mansfield being Mouse,[21] the author said in that same letter that "there's so much much less taken from life than anybody would credit."

In many ways, the story sounds like Mansfield's version of *The Waste Land*, appearing some two years prior to Eliot's. It also sound like another of Eliot's poems, and although demonstrating that Mansfield must have got part of "the bloody thing from" Eliot's "The Love Song of J. Alfred Prufrock" is not going to solve all the mystery of this story, it may shed a little more light on a complex piece of fiction. Within days after Eliot's poem was published in June 1917, Mansfield read it aloud at a party, and Marvin Magalaner has seen Eliot's influence in the Prufrockian characters of "Bliss" (1918).[22] Echoes of lines from this poem have previously been noted in other portions of Mansfield's writing,[23] but the echoes in *Je ne parle pas français* are louder than anywhere else.

As the "you and I" of Eliot's poem are conventionally read to be two sides of Prufrock's personality, so Duquette's statement that "I had shown somebody both sides of my life" is but one instance in the confessions of a divided personality. Prufrock's monologue is certainly also confessional. Thus the narrators of the two works appear to be of much the same nature, although Prufrock does not admit to being as cynical as Duquette, who, in turn, tries to pretend that he is not as sentimental as Prufrock.

Were it not for the many words and phrases in Mansfield's story that echo those from Eliot's poem, however, the basic similarities of the narrators might not be noticed. Parallel lists will perhaps best demonstrate the similarities in language:

Mansfield's story	*Eliot's poem*
"the Ultimate Porter"	"the eternal Footman"
"That's not exactly what I mean"	"That is not what I meant at all"
the waiter strews straw on floor	"sawdust restaurants"
it has such a "dying fall"	"voices dying with a dying fall"
"I hadn't a phrase to meet it with"	"fix you in a formulated phrase"
"those fogs"	"the yellow fog"
"those endless streets"	"streets that follow like a tedious argument"
"dressed with particular care for the occasion"	"My necktie rich and modest, but asserted by a simple pin"
"ran down the stairs"	"descend the stair"
wants to behave "like a clown"	"Almost, at times, the Fool"

Part 1

Mansfield's story	Eliot's poem
"faced with a great crisis"	"to force the moment to its crisis"
people "leaning out" of windows	"men in shirt-sleeves leaning out of windows"
"new morning coat"	"my morning coat"

Two longer quotations also show that Mansfield must have had many of the sounds and ideas of Eliot's poem rattling around in her mind while she wrote her story: "Her voice was quite calm, but it was not her voice any more. It was like the voice you might imagine coming out of a tiny, cold sea-shell swept high and dry at last by the salt tide" (*KM*, 375); and "We have lingered in the chambers of the sea/By sea-girls wreathed with seaweed red and brown/Till human voices wake us, and we drown."[24]

Mansfield, as other readers have said, may have been doing several things in this story. Alpers says that the story is "in some measure a riposte to Carco's *Les Innocents*"; he also credits its writing to "three main impulses": Mansfield's "irrational loathing" for the French, "her profound despair about the war and what it was doing to everything she loved," and "her love for Jack." For Alpers, that last impulse was the strongest, and he cites as evidence Mansfield's writing to Murry that "she had 'fed on our love' as she wrote it, and she called it a tribute to Love, you understand, and the best that I can do just now'" (Alpers, 270).

Seeing *Je ne parle pas français* in all these dimensions does not keep us from seeing it also as some kind of response to ideas and emotions expressed in Eliot's poem. Mansfield not only endorses and reinforces the despair over the loss of love—of the inability to love and to communicate spiritually through love with fellow human beings that is so much a part of both "The Love Song of J. Alfred Prufrock" and *The Waste Land*—but goes beyond Eliot's earlier poem and may even go beyond his later one in the depth of despair, in the bitterness displayed about the treatment of Mouse by both men. Her cry may echo Eliot's in "Prufrock," but it precedes his *The Waste Land* and may even exceed it in terms of strong emotions more directly and immediately expressed, because Mansfield's form makes her bitterness and depth of passion, her "cry against corruption," more accessible to more readers than does Eliot's allusion-loaded and footnote-burdened form.

The Nervous Characters

A number of Mansfield's stories concern nervous characters or tense situations. Of three stories about characters whose nerves are of primary concern, two portray women ("Revelations" and "The Escape") and one portrays a man ("Mr. Reginald Peacock's Day"). Tense and terribly "modern" relationships between a man and a woman occur in three other stories: "Psychology," "A Dill Pickle," and "Poison." Probably the best of these stories about life among the excitable moderns is "Bliss."

Monica Tyrell in "Revelations" provides an excellent example of a woman who suffers "from her nerves." At age thirty-three Monica suffers every morning from eight until "about half-past eleven" (*KM*, 425). On the morning of the particular action of the story she is awakened far too early by her maid, Marie, banging into the bedroom to throw open the blinds and the curtains. Then Monica's husband, Ralph, is on the telephone to see if she "will lunch at Princes' at one-thirty" (*KM*, 426). Given that it is only nine-thirty, Monica swears at him in her mind: "How dared Ralph do such a thing when he knew how agonizing her nerves were in the morning!" (*KM*, 426). She does manage to pull herself together, however, and heads out in a taxi anywhere it may take her. Since her husband has proved once again that he does not understand her, Monica heads for her hairdresser's because everyone in the shop loves and understands "the real her" (*KM*, 428). Mansfield's most unsubstantial characters most often believe in real selves that struggle bravely toward the surface. Monica, together with Kezia's Aunt Beryl, is a case in point.

Monica is, unfortunately, baffled by the actions of both Madame, apparently the proprietor, and "George who did her hair." Madame barely greets her and has a strange "note in her voice"; George smiles in a strange way, seems unshaven, and does not say anything nice about her hair. Eventually George tells Monica that his first child, a daughter, has died that morning. Monica rushes out of the shop to her taxi, demands that she be taken to Princes', and on the way, while passing a flower shop, thinks about sending flowers signed "From an unknown friend. . . . From one who understands" (*KM*, 431). But the driver does not hear her tap on the window, "and, anyway, they were at Princes' already."

Thus this slight story ends with Monica's failure to perform an unselfish act. Were she really able to send the flowers, the story implies, her husband might be able to take her seriously; as things are, she gives him no reason to do so. One of the weaknesses of the story is Mansfield's resting her case against Monica on an outside occurrence, one not intrinsic to her personality. Probably most readers can take Monica no more seriously than her husband does; she really seems to have so little trouble accepting her own selfishness that she is not worth paying attention to. Mansfield suggests that selfishness may be the essence of the "real" Monica, but that is hardly what the woman herself considers to be at the heart of her personality.

An almost hysterical woman is the center of attention and the active consciousness in "The Escape," which begins with her berating her husband, mentally, for his inept handling of their departure from a hotel and their attempt to take a train. Of his performance, which the reader has no objective way of estimating, she thinks, "Oh, why am I made to bear these things?" Later, in a horse-drawn vehicle she complains about "the disgusting, revolting dust" (*KM*, 432) and reacts strongly to her husband's suggestion that she put up her parasol: "And anyone who was not utterly insensitive would know that I'm far, far too exhausted to hold up a parasol" (*KM*, 433). Her tirade continues as she attacks him for forgetting that she cannot stand for him to smoke when they "are driving together" (*KM*, 434). Her parasol falls out of the carriage, and she insists on walking back to look for it, saying to her husband, "If I don't escape from you for a minute I shall go mad" (*KM*, 435).

At this point the story switches into the husband's consciousness, and in another echo of lines from Eliot he thinks of himself as "lying there, a hollow man, a parched, withered man, as it were, of ashes."[25] Seeing a tree "just inside a garden gate," the man apparently has some sort of mystical experience in which he sees "something beyond the tree—a whiteness, a softness, an opaque mass, half-hidden—with delicate pillars." The singing voice of a woman floats "upon the air, and it was all part of the silence as he was part of it" (*KM*, 435). Mansfield describes what is happening to the man in these words: "Something stirred in his breast. Something dark, something unbearable and dreadful pushed in his bosom, and like a great weed it floated, rocked . . .

it was warm, stifling. He tried to struggle to tear at it, and at the same moment—all was over. Deep, deep, he sank into the silence, staring at the tree and waiting for the voice that came floating, falling, until he felt himself enfolded" (*KM*, 435–36). This description sounds a good deal more like death by heart attack than a mystical experience. This reading is supported by the abrupt and major break in the story, signaled by a series of dots, which appears right after the above-quoted passage.

When the story begins again with the sentence fragment "In the shaking corridor of the train" (*KM*, 436), surely most readers are baffled by Mansfield's implication that all the events in the horse-drawn vehicle did not really occur but were part of someone's imagination. When does this couple board the train? Where in the narrative is there any indication that the train ride is actual and the carriage ride a fantasy or hallucination? The reader who returns to the earlier pages of the story may well continue to be baffled about exactly what is going on here. The scope of the problem for the reader can be demonstrated only by quoting the last three paragraphs of the story, all coming after the major break and the husband's experience quoted above:

> In the shaking corridor of the train. It was night. The train rushed and roared through the dark. He held on with both hands to the brass rail. The door of their carriage was open.
>
> "Do not disturb yourself, Monsieur. He will come in and sit down when he wants to. He likes—he likes—it is his habit. . . . *Oui, Madame, je suis un peu souffrante. . . . Mes nerfs*. Oh, but my husband is never so happy as when he is travelling. He likes roughing it. . . . My husband. . . . My husband. . . ."
>
> The voices murmured, murmured. They were never still. But so great was his heavenly happiness as he stood there he wished that he might live for ever. (*KM*, 436)

Surely all the third-person-masculine pronouns must refer to the woman's husband, but what is his condition? Her stammering words reflect pain about his status or condition. The last paragraph, in the reference to the voices, seems to take the husband back to his mystical or death experience in the carriage. The words *heavenly happiness* may, again, be a suggestion of death, but how can that have occurred if he is standing in the corridor of a railroad carriage? And who is the other man that the woman addresses? It sounds as if this man is trying to get the husband to go into the compartment and sit down, perhaps because he seems to be sick. If this other man speaks to the woman in French, why does Mansfield make it an interruption of the woman's speech, without any conventional quotation marks around it? And why does this other man speak of his suffering from nerves?

Frankly, I do not have reasonable answers, nor have I found any other writer about Mansfield who has explained what is literally going on at the end of this story. The story may not be worth additional study, but how can any reader know that before the study is made and the questions are answered?

The title character of "Mr. Reginald Peacock's Day" joins Monica Tyrell in being a terribly sensitive person who cannot stand to be awakened in the morning. The unidentified woman who gloats "over her triumph" in getting him up turns out to be his wife, who, Reginald thinks, is "denying him his rights as an artist, by trying to drag him down to her level" (*KM*, 384). Reginald's art is singing, but his livelihood apparently comes from giving voice lessons to simpering women of no talent, each of whom he addresses as "Dear Lady." The story prances Reginald through a series of lessons, deposits him at a dinner party to sing triumphantly, and sends him staggering home after too much wine. Wishing that his "enemy, even in her sleep" were someone he could confide in, someone who would share his triumphs, Reginald awakens his wife by hurling "his evening boot" into the corner. He wants to make "one more try to treat her as a friend, to tell her everything, to win her," but when he sits down on the bed, "for some fiendish reason" all he can utter is the phony sentence he has been saying all day to his phony students: "Dear Lady, I should be so charmed—so charmed!" (*KM*, 392).

Mansfield clearly paints Reginald far too broadly with her satirical brush for this story to be listed as one of her best. It is told almost entirely through Reginald's consciousness, and Mansfield too obviously undermines his story with his own excessive exaggerations and poses. It is fun watching Mansfield shoot him down, but she is also the one who set him up as such an easy target to hit. Because Reginald is pictured as such a precious pretender to art, the story cannot seriously wrestle with the one of the major questions Mansfield often asked of herself: Are romantic artists really different from other people?

"Psychology" may be more a clinical examination of psychological games than it is a story of the unnamed man and woman who play one. The primary point of view can be called dualistic, because much of the time the narration is reflecting that they think identically about their relationship, as the following sentences demonstrate: "And the best of it was they were both of them old enough to enjoy their adventure to the full without any stupid emotional complication. Passion would have ruined everything; they quite saw that" (*KM*, 316). Shortly after his surprise arrival at her place just in time for tea, "their secret selves" (*KM*, 314) whisper a series of five statements about their relationship; in not distinguishing one speaker from the other, Mansfield shows that both think they are thinking the same thing. The clinician's role that Mansfield is playing here demonstrates that psychologically no two people can think as one.

Although in opening the paragraph Mansfield allows the man and woman to think jointly that "the special thrilling quality of their friendship was in their complete surrender," when she ends the paragraph she does it with their jointly held belief that this friendship has "made it possible for him to be utterly truthful to her and for her to be utterly sincere with him" (*KM*, 316). The differences in meaning between *truthful* and *sincere* proclaim Mansfield's psychological truth that the two characters cannot be thinking and feeling in unison, as they shape their own feelings in reaction to those expressed in the psychological novel they are reading. Mansfield almost seems to be playing her own game with their feelings. I read these characters as totally serious, with neither playing a conscious game of manipulation, unlike Anne in "Mr. and Mrs. Dove." These two are more deluded than deluding. They quickly start a conversation after a silence has come between them, and their supposedly dual thought process goes like this: "They were off and all was as usual. But was it? Weren't they just a little too quick, too prompt with their replies, too ready to take each other up? Was this really anything more than a wonderfully good imitation of other occasions?" (*KM*, 317–18). What is so wonderful about Mansfield's performance here is that she makes them together question their ability to be together, while also suggesting that on those "other occasions" they were not any more together than they are now, even though they may have thought they were.

Once again a "silence put a spell upon them like solemn music," showing that they really do not have the relationship they think they do. Real friends can be quiet together. He breaks the silence by saying that he must keep an appointment, to which "her secret self" (note that it is not their common secret selves quoted earlier) thinks, "We've failed!" Although she, with apparent clinical accuracy, puts the blame on both of them for failing, her subsequent thoughts shift the blame completely onto the man. Her heart cries to itself, "You've hurt me—hurt me. Why don't you go? No, don't go. Stay. No—go" (*KM*, 319). After he does go, she flings herself around her studio, crying out, "How stupid! How imbecile!" (*KM*, 320), but Mansfield never tells us who has been so stupid as to do what. Again Mansfield sends the man away, so that the reader does not get to learn his reaction to the scene. After thinking that she will never see him again and that she should just let the doorbell ringing go unanswered, the woman flies to the door.

Standing there is "an elderly virgin, a pathetic creature who simply idolized her" (*KM*, 320) and regularly shows up with cheap and often wilted flowers. At first, not taking today's violets and not saying anything, the woman feels "the silence that was like a question." Moving forward carefully "as though fearful of making a ripple in that boundless pool of quiet she put her arms round her friend" (*KM*, 320), who is described as feeling so "tenderly" "enfolded" that her "mind positively reeled" (*KM*, 321). Now when she goes back to her studio, she feels "so light, so rested, as if she had woken up out of a childish sleep. Even the act of breathing was a joy."

Although the story ends with the woman's writing a note to her male friend, suggesting that he come back to continue their "talk about the psychological novel" (*KM*, 321), Mansfield's story has resoundingly stated that the feelings generated between two women by the sincere gift of almost-dead violets and an equally sincere giving of oneself in an embrace mean a great deal more than the psychological maneuvering between a man and a woman over the psychological novel, which is what brings them together in the first place.

As "Psychology" ends in the woman's consciousness, so "A Dill Pickle" starts in Vera's, as, in a restaurant, she recognizes an old love from six years ago. At first, neither seems very much changed, as he still plays "the trick of interrupting her" and she still says "the same things" and still has her "beautiful way of speaking" (*KM*, 331). They remember together the things they did, and he does a great deal more talking than she does, telling her, with just the slightest hint of bragging, of all the foreign places he has been to, which they once dreamed together of visiting. She seems to have gone down financially while he has gone up from the time they were poor together. Their conversation, however, in its general tenor seems to be going well, with none of the emotional pressures visible between the couple in "Psychology."

Then he recounts an episode from his Russian travel in which a coachman had offered him a dill pickle because "he wanted to share with us. That seemed to me so right, so—you know what I mean?" After imagining herself in that Russian scene, she says, "Yes, I know perfectly what you mean" (*KM*, 334). The ensuing passage resembles some of those in "Psychology" that have to do with whether one person really can know "perfectly" what another means. (The reader should be reminded that Mansfield in no way questions Laurie Sheridan's ability to understand what his sister means in "The Garden Party.") In "A Dill Pickle" Mansfield not only questions the characters' present ability to be soul mates but also, in the tone of the following words, seems to question the truth of the feelings they remember having in the past: "In the pause that followed they looked at each other. In the past when they had looked at each other like that they had felt such a boundless understanding between them that their souls had, as it were, put their arms around each other and dropped into the same sea, content to be drowned, like mournful lovers" (*KM*, 334–35).

This time when he breaks the silence, to tell her how wonderful a listener she is, she hears "just a hint of mockery in his voice" (*KM*, 335), or at least fancies that she does. As he talks about the letter she wrote that apparently put an end to their earlier relationship and says that her "clever" letter painted "a true picture" of him, she knows he is mocking her. She starts to leave, but he begs her to stay. He does a little trick of drawing her glove through his fingers, making him look "more like himself of six years ago." When he begins to tell her about the nature of his earlier feelings, "the strange beast in her bosom began to purr. . . ." and as he continues, she thinks to herself, "Ah, God! What had she done! How had she dared to throw way her happiness like this. This was the only man who had ever understood her" (*KM*, 336). Mansfield pictures the woman as being taken in by this man's smooth ways. He seems to mesmerize her with his words and his "stroking the glove," even without her hand in it, until she feels that she is "that glove that he held in his fingers" (*KM*, 336).

Why, having put her into this state, he suddenly hands her glove back to her and scrapes "his chair on the floor" is a matter for the reader's interpretation. The accumulated evidence from many stories suggests that Mansfield is saying that this man does just what men almost invariably do in such cases: They simply walk out, and they especially like to do that when they sense their loss of control of the situation or are about to make a commitment they believe they cannot afford to make. Whatever the reason, he clearly extricates himself by saying that the old feelings he once considered mysterious he now understands to have been selfishness, egotism; he says the two of them were "so wrapped up" in themselves that they had no room in their hearts for anyone else. As he talks, she leaves and he is "thunderstruck." When he gets his bill, he asks the waitress not to charge him for the cream, because it "has not been touched" (*KM*, 337). With this final touch, Mansfield says, without doubt, that he has accurately described his selfish male egotism. Because he is finally made to look so bad, Vera is made to look better.

In "A Dill Pickle" Mansfield has again loaded the sympathy onto the woman. But she has carefully—and because of the nature of her narrative style—removed any authorial voice that would lead the reader directly to the "truth" about Vera's personality and motives. Is Vera really as selfish as the man? As in so many of these stories, each reader must find whatever there is to be found only in the words, thoughts, and actions of the characters themselves.

Rounding out different narrative perspectives, "Poison" is told through the mind of a male narrator whose point of view is best described as thinking about the events as they occur in the present. Of course, such a narrative perspective cannot really be achieved, but this narrator is certainly not telling the story with any kind of judgmental stance after the fact. Again, the story represents Mansfield's blend of the immediacy of a stage performance with the internal point of view of one of the actors on the stage. It cannot happen, but it does. The story is like a soliloquy without the rest of the stage performances around it.

Like the majority of the males in Mansfield's stories about these modern liaisons, the narrator of "Poison" has no name, a fact that lends credence to the belief that Mansfield really did believe that the men of her generation were all alike—unless, of course, they were so different as to be named Reginald, as in Peacock and "Mr. and Mrs. Dove." This narrator, however, perhaps ought to have a name, because he seems to embody more of the loving and caring sensitivity of Henry in "Something Childish but Very Natural" than he does the hurtful men of "A Dill Pickle" and "Psychology."

The woman who wears only "one pearl ring—no wedding ring" on her left hand is named Beatrice, and her lover—the narrator—thinks that the two of them are finding supreme bliss together, apparently in the south of France. The narrator says that he agrees outwardly with Beatrice that they need not pretend to be married, but "privately, in the depths of my heart, I would have given my soul to have stood beside her" in an old-fashioned wedding "with old reverend clergy-men" (*KM*, 565). He admits that he desires such a wedding not because he cares "for such horrible shows, but because I felt it might possibly perhaps lessen this ghastly feeling of absolute freedom, *her* absolute freedom, of course" (*KM*, 566).

Beatrice's elusiveness echoes that of Edna, created seven years earlier with Henry in "Something Childish but Very Natural." In fact, Beatrice sings the first two lines of the Coleridge poem about being a bird and flying away that plays such a major role in the earlier story, thereby implying her own desire to fly away. In response to her singing, the narrator asks her to assure him that she will not leave him. She jokingly says that she will go no farther than "the bottom of the road" (*KM*, 566), to check on the mail, in whose arrival she seems to have an undue interest. When they do see the mailman coming up the hill, Beatrice describes him as looking "like a blue beetle," which provides another connection with "Something Childish." Henry, at the conclusion of that story, sees the girl bringing the fatal telegram to him as being a white moth. Thus seven years later, Mansfield seems to have had some of the same feelings about a sincere and loving young man (this one is only twenty-four) being hurt by a woman who is not nearly so happy in their relationship as he is.

If "Poison" echoes Mansfield's own earlier story, it also suggests John Keats's "Ode on a Grecian Urn" in its emphasis on the ethereal emotional moment and on the torture of being so happy that one cannot help but know that the moment cannot last. The man here states these feelings this way: "What torture happiness was—what anguish!" (*KM*, 566). When Beatrice reassures him that she has "never been so happy as I have these last two months," he feels "such bliss—it was so extraordinary, so unprecedented, to hear her talk like this that I had to try to laugh it off" (*KM*, 567). He feels that he must lessen the degree of happiness in order to lessen his pain when it inevitably comes. He senses that what he has to look forward to are "a heart high-sorrowful and cloy'd,/A burning forehead, and a parching tongue."[26] The postman brings only a newspaper, which Beatrice characterizes as having nothing in it, "only some poison trial." He, too, tries to keep the outside world, reality, away from their idyllic world by "flinging" the paper "into another chair," thinking, "I wanted to forget the paper, to return, but cautiously, of course, to that moment before the postman came. But when she answered I knew from her voice the moment was over for now" (*KM*, 568). The news of the trial causes Beatrice to discuss at length the poisoning of mates and lovers and to make Mansfield's point that a relationship itself is as subject to poisoning as a person is. Beatrice's laughing assertion that couples "*survive*" only "because the one is frightened of giving the other a fatal dose" is followed by her statement that "Both my husbands poisoned me" (*KM*, 569). Although it sounds as if she could be talking about literal poisonings, what Mansfield really means is that Beatrice is blaming her husbands for poisoning her ability to survive in a relationship. The man tries to tell her that the things that happened to her with her two husbands were the result of her being "too perfect for this horrible world—too exquisite, too fine. It frightened people. I made a little joke" (*KM*, 569).

A number of points can be made about what the man says here. One is that he—like Henry in "Something Childish," who thinks of Edna as perfect—is wrong. Beatrice is not perfect; no one is, of course. The second is that his thinking that he is truly making a "little joke" means that he really is not joking and truly does conduct himself in this relationship with the false belief that she is perfect. Thus he poisons the relationship. The third point is that many readers may be reminded of Nathaniel Hawthorne's story "The Birthmark," in which the husband tries to remove a birthmark from his wife's face in order to make her perfect. In his attempt, he does administer "the fatal dose," and she dies. The reader should know at this point in Mansfield's story that the idyllic relationship is poisoned and dead.

Continuing with an ambiguity about responsibilities and causes and effects that would make Hawthorne proud, Mansfield causes Beatrice to say to her lover in response to his assertion that he has not tried to poison her, "You wouldn't hurt a fly!" To these words he responds, in his thoughts, "Strange. That hurt, though. Most horribly" (*KM*, 569). Has Beatrice administered the final dose of poison to his love for her? They are interrupted by Annette, the maid, who brings them drinks before lunch. As they drink, the man tries to explain that Beatrice, rather than poisoning people, fills them up "with new life," with "something of her own radiance" (*KM*, 570). Of course, she kills this thought by asking him to go to the post office after lunch to see whether any letters have arrived, even though she insists she is not expecting any. The story ends and says that the relationship has ended by poisoning, with the man "thinking of—postmen and blue beetles and farewells that were not farewells and . . . Good God! Was it fancy? No, it wasn't fancy. The drink tasted chill, bitter, *queer*" (*KM*, 570).

Bliss seems to come upon thirty-year-old Bertha Young in "Bliss" almost in the way that God's grace is believed to come upon a person: unearned, unsought, unexplained. Bertha is merely "turning the corner" of her own street when she is "overcome, suddenly, by a feeling of bliss—absolute bliss!" (*KM*, 337). Mansfield's story never directly explains this "almost unbearable" feeling, this "bright glowing place" in Bertha's bosom, this feeling of "waiting for something . . . divine to happen . . . that she knew must happen . . . infallibly" (*KM*, 338). Bertha herself, of course, eventually does try to explain it, in terms of all the fine things she enjoys in this world: money; "an adorable baby"; a husband who loves her, gets on well with her, and is her pal; an "absolutely satisfactory house and garden"; and "modern, thrilling friends" (*KM*, 342). As if this potpourri of false reasons is not sufficient to sink Bertha's reasoning of its own weight, Mansfield caps the whole things off with a new cook who makes "the most superb omelettes . . ." (*KM*, 342). Bertha follows her listing of the reasons for her bliss with the statement to herself "I'm absurd. Absurd!" She then tells herself it "must have been the spring" (*KM*, 342).

Here Mansfield causes Bertha to state the possible truth about her feelings, although she probably does not really believe what she says. Her feeling of bliss is as natural as the sap rising in the spring, as normal in a woman as the flowering of the pear tree in the Youngs' garden. When much later in the story Bertha "for the first time in her life" desires her husband in a sexual way and thinks about how "at first" in the marriage she worried "dreadfully" about the fact "that she was so cold" (*KM*, 348), Mansfield reveals the truth of the matter. But she also allows Bertha to denigrate these natural yearnings by saying that she and Harry have found that her sexual coldness does not seem to matter, because they are "so frank with each other—such good pals. That was the best of being modern" (*KM*, 348). Moderns of the sort who attend the Youngs' dinner party that night have moved beyond these childish and natural feelings that might very well arise, even in a thirty-year-old married lady, in the spring "when the world is puddle-wonderful." But just as E. E. Cummings's poem also contains the threat of "the goat-footed balloonMan,"[27] so, too, will Mansfield's story put an end to Bertha's bliss with her discovery of an affair between Harry and one of the dinner guests, Miss Fulton.

But before that discovery occurs, Mansfield indicates by Bertha's actions toward her friends at the dinner party that being struck by natural bliss does not mean, at least in Bertha Young's case, that a person is going to be so freed of conventions (modern or otherwise) as to be able to shout out in a natural, truthful, and childish way that the king is not wearing any clothes. Obviously, the guests at the Youngs' party, their very "modern, thrilling friends," need someone to point out that they are in altogether very bad taste. Mansfield, despite Bertha's approving attitude about them, surely can leave no doubt in any reader's mind that these characters are the subject of her authorial laughter. Mrs. Norman Knight is wearing "the most amusing orange coat with a procession of black monkeys round the hem and up the fronts" (*KM*, 342). Eddie Warren dresses his conversation with italicized words: "I have had such a *dreadful* experience with a taxi-man; he was *most* sinister. I couldn't get him to *stop*" (*KM*, 343). Mr. Norman Knight presses "a large tortoiseshell-rimmed monocle into his eye" (*KM*, 342). Bertha's condition does not cause her to see any of this as folly and foolishness. Her own bliss might cause her to see their folly, if she really understood its source. But having explained away to herself the natural source of her bliss, she can go on thinking of Eddie Warren as an attractive person. Of course, in making Bertha so obtuse to all this modern foolishness, Mansfield runs considerable risk of undermining the sense she has created in the story that Bertha's feeling of bliss is natural and positive. Yet the reader is apparently expected to take Bertha seriously, especially in feeling sympathetic toward her when Bertha discovers her husband's infidelity.

Prior to making that discovery, however, Bertha's strong feelings of happiness cause her to misread Miss Fulton very badly. Bertha clearly is looking for someone to share her bliss. Earlier she has tried to share it with her baby daughter, but in feeding and cuddling the baby "all her feeling of bliss came back again, and again she didn't know how to express it—what to do with it" (*KM*, 340). Thus when Pearl Fulton, whom Bertha has previously said she likes a great deal, although Harry has said she suffers from "anaemia of the brain" (*KM*, 341), asks the apparently innocuous question of Bertha, "Have you a garden?" Bertha takes it as "the sign" (*KM*, 346) that Pearl has picked up Bertha's blissful vibrations and is ready to share them with her. They go to the window and look out at the pear tree in blossom in the moonlight. Bertha completely transmits her feelings onto Miss Fulton. Mansfield includes nothing in the description of the scene to suggest that Pearl sees anything as Bertha sees it or shares any of these emotions:

> How long did they stand there? Both, as it were, caught in that circle of unearthly light, understanding each other perfectly, creatures of another world, and wondering what they were to do in this one with all this blissful treasure that burned in their bosoms and dropped, in silver flowers, from their hair and hands?
>
> For ever—for a moment? And did Miss Fulton murmur: "Yes. Just *that*." Or did Bertha dream it? (*KM*, 347)

Mansfield achieves wonderful irony in the story, first by causing this imagined empathy from Miss Fulton to be part of the reason that Bertha at last desires her husband and then by throwing Harry Young and Pearl Fulton into an embrace. The ambiguity of all these emotions, the great difficulty every reader has in knowing what Mansfield feels and wants the reader to feel about modern marriage pals, sexual desires in women (perhaps even for other women), modernism in its many manifestations, and feelings of unexpected bliss—all this is caught in Bertha's closing cry, "Oh, what is going to happen now?" (*KM*, 350). Bertha certainly does not know; if Mansfield knew, she didn't say; a reader can only make some guesses and draw some tentative conclusions.

Meanwhile, "the pear tree was as lovely as ever and as full of flower and as still" (*KM*, 350). Life, whatever it is and whatever it means, goes on. Nature is always there, and in it humans, in fact and fiction, keep trying to determine exactly what it means for a human to be natural, to find the right way for humans to live. Rather than stating how to live, rather than being philosophical about what life means, Katherine Mansfield's short stories offer many pictures of how some characters have lived. Many of those characters seek answers in the same way Mansfield did in her own life, and all the answers they find are as tentative as all she personally found.

I think that in some important ways Bertha Young's reaction to the onset of bliss in "Bliss" resembles what a conscientious reader of that story (and many other Mansfield stories) can experience: Bertha definitely feels what is happening to her, but she cannot discover the source of her bliss or account for why it has arrived on this particular occasion. A first-time reader of a Mansfield story may have similar feelings of bliss while experiencing the story and may well not understand their source. Why does this story on this reading create such pleasure for this particular reader? Literary criticism, of course, cannot answer that question.

The quotation from John Middleton Murry with which I began the Preface addresses the question of why and how a Mansfield story can produce aesthetic bliss. The causes cannot be reduced to a formula, but they can be talked about in regard to individual stories. I have tried in this book to demonstrate some reasons that certain stories produced bliss for me and to show that often a Mansfield story succeeds in wedding aesthetic beauty and truth into the oneness that John Keats claimed for them in his famous poetic assertion that "beauty is truth, truth beauty." Mansfield would not disagree with this claim by her fellow romantic artist. Her previously quoted statement that she did not get "the deepest truth" out of the story "An Ideal Family" means that the story lacks beauty, is not the success she wanted it to be. Because it lacks beauty (is not good enough) it is lacking in truth. For the romantic artist like Mansfield, truth lies in beauty; it does not reside elsewhere.

In contrast to "An Ideal Family," a story such as "The Daughters of the Late Colonel" creates truth and beauty for me, even if the bliss felt is that common but unexplainable aesthetic pleasure that we somehow enjoy because of (certainly not despite) the obvious sufferings of the characters. Bertha Young enjoys her bliss but at the same time is greatly pained because she cannot fathom its source, which means that she does not know how to produce it again. Nor can I reproduce the bliss I felt during a given reading of a story. I cannot simply enjoy bliss in reading about the constrained Pinner sisters; I must suffer to some degree their confined and narrow lives with them. A reader who cannot do that (whatever the reason) cannot see the beauty and truth of how Mansfield depicts those lives. The reasons for a reader's inability to feel some degree of empathy for Constantia and Josephine must lie within the person; they cannot lie in the story, or the story would not have been capable of transmitting its signals of beauty and truth to any reader. Those signals will never be the same, nor will they always produce the same results in any given reader. The degree of beauty and truth will change on every reading; perhaps even the name applied to their effect will change every time. How a Mansfield story works depends, of course, on how the story works. That is not a tautology but a truth.

Some of Mansfield's finest, most beautiful, and most truthful stories, such as "The Garden Party," "The Doll's House," and "The Young Girl," fascinate the adult reader because they re-create with fidelity what it once meant to be young and vulnerable and honest to our emotions. The ennui, the competition, the self-serving qualities of courtship and marriage that occur in "Marriage à la Mode," "Mr. and Mrs. Dove," and "A Cup of Tea" are beautiful and truthful in more painful and adult ways. That Mansfield remained able to feel like a child, see like an adult, and write like an angel is one of the great mysteries of imaginative creativity. Mansfield probably did not see life through a "crystal-clear" lens, as Murry claimed, but she did imagine fictional lives of long duration out of her own short-lived and often painful existence.

Anthologies being assembled seventy years after Mansfield's death will continue to contain her stories. The modernist period of which Mansfield was so much a part and which she so well represents has been replaced by the not-at-all-well-named postmodern period. Mansfield's stories, however, are irreplaceable. They will continue to "tease us out of thought/as doth eternity." The bliss that readers will continue to feel will remain "for ever young/All breathing human passion far above." The stories will remain beyond our ability to explain but always just within our ability to enjoy.

Notes to Part 1

1. Antony Alpers, *The Life of Katherine Mansfield* (New York: Viking Press, 1980), 92–95. Hereafter cited in text as Alpers.

2. *The Short Stories of Katherine Mansfield* (New York: Knopf, 1937), 37. Hereafter cited in text as *KM*.

3. The similarities between Mansfield's "The Child-Who-Was-Tired" and Anton Chekhov's "Sleepyhead" were first pointed out by Elisabeth Schneider ("Katherine Mansfield and Chekhov," *Modern Language Notes* 50 [1935] : 394–97). Although probably not the last word, one of the more convincing interpretations of the relationship between the stories is that of Ronald Sutherland in "Katherine Mansfield: Plagiarist, Disciple, or Ardent Admirer?" (*Critique* 5 [1962] : 58–75).

4. *The Letters of Katherine Mansfield*, ed. J. Middleton Murry (New York: Knopf, 1929), 296. Hereafter cited in text as *Letters*.

5. Although "The Aloe" was subsequently published in book form (1982), it is conventionally considered a short story. *Prelude* was originally published in book form (1918) and is usually called a novel, although it is shorter than most novels. Mansfield at one time intended to expand this "novel" about the Burnell family.

6. *The Collected Letters of Katherine Mansfield*, vol. 1, 1903–17, ed. Vincent O'Sullivan and Margaret Scott (Oxford: Oxford University Press, 1984), 167. Hereafter cited in text as O'Sullivan.

7. *Journal of Katherine Mansfield*, "Definitive Edition," ed. J. Middleton Murry (London: Constable & Co., 1954), 94. Hereafter cited in text as *Journal*.

8. *The Portable James Joyce*, ed. Harry Levin (New York: Viking Press, 1947), 19, 29.

9. Kate Fullbrook, *Katherine Mansfield* (Bloomington: Indiana University Press, 1986), 51. Hereafter cited in text as Fullbrook.

10. The fidelity pledged in Robert Burns's "A Red, Red Rose" to love "while the sands o'life shall run" is certainly stronger than Isabel's.

11. For an extended comparison not only of "The Stranger" and "The Dead" but of Mansfield's and Joyce's short story artistry in general, see Sylvia Berkman, *Katherine Mansfield: A Critical Study* (New Haven: Yale University Press, 1951), 159–74.

12. Saralyn Daly, *Katherine Mansfield* (New York: Twayne Publishers, 1965), 80.

13. D. H. Lawrence, *Sons and Lovers* (New York: Modern Library, n.d.), 205.

14. Ernest Hemingway, *The Sun Also Rises* (New York: Modern Library, n.d.), 153.

15. Mansfield wrote to Murry (*Collected Letters*, 2:54) that her two "kick offs" for writing were joy and "an extremely deep sense of hopelessness of everything doomed to disaster" while in the middle of writing *Je ne parle pas français*, a book she described as "a cry against corruption."

16. Clare Hanson and Andrew Gurr, *Katherine Mansfield* (New York: St. Martin's Press, 1981), 93. Hereafter cited in text as Hanson and Gurr.

17. For Lesley Moore's (née Ida Baker) version of their relationship, see *Katherine Mansfield: The Memories of LM* (London: Michael Joseph, 1971).

18. The first line of "East Coker" (T. S. Eliot, *Four Quartets* [New York: Harcourt, Brace & Co., 1943], 11).

19. Gerard Manley Hopkins, "Spring and Fall: To a Young Child," line 14.

20. J. F. Kobler, "The Sexless Narrator of Mansfield's 'The Young Girl,'" *Studies in Short Fiction* 17 (Summer 1980) : 269–74.

21. J. Middleton Murry, *Between Two Worlds: An Autobiography* (London: Jonathan Cape, 1935), 463.

22. Alpers, *Life of Katherine Mansfield*, 239; Marvin Magalaner, *The Fiction of Katherine Mansfield* (Carbondale: Southern Illinois University Press, 1971), 85.

23. Of a statement about her inability to complete some stories, Mansfield said, in the late summer of 1917, "That is not what I meant at all," which is precisely a line used twice by Eliot (Murry, *Journal of Katherine Mansfield*, 124).

24. All quotations from "The Love Song of J. Alfred Prufrock" are from *The American Tradition in Literature*, 6th ed., ed. George Perkins et. al (New York: Random House, 1985), 1066–69.

25. Eliot's poem "The Hollow Men" begins with the line "We are the hollow men" and speaks of their "dried voices" (Perkins et al., *The American Tradition*, 1086).

26. John Keats, "Ode on a Grecian Urn," ll. 29–30.

27. The bliss of being a child in spring is caught wonderfully in E. E. Cummings's poem "In Just—/spring."

Part 2

THE WRITER

Introduction

From early in her life until her death, Katherine Mansfield felt the drive to be an "artist" in almost every sense of the word as it has been used since the beginnings of the romantic revolution at the turn of the nineteenth century. The artist is different from ordinary persons, having a much greater sensitivity to the world around her; the artist recognizes the necessary relationship that exists between the human being and the rest of nature. Out of this sensitivity to and close relationship with nature grows a kind of art that reveals more ultimate and higher truths about the human condition on this planet than any other form of human activity, with the possible exception of those rare religious activities that are pursued with an equal purity of spirit, acceptance of beauty, and freedom of individual conscience. Mansfield not only believed that these basic conditions of the romantic artist existed in her, but she accepted, sometimes with a struggle, the results of being such an artist in a literary world that is not fundamentally different from other human social institutions. The romantic artist is made constantly aware of the fact that her pursuit of her own truth and beauty through art must be in competition with the pursuits of other artists for literary success and favors. Likewise, her pursuit of the highest and purest forms of perfection in all things (writing, loving, living) is in constant conflict with *the* world and with societal worlds that regularly settle for a good deal less than supernal truth and beauty. Mansfield realized that she had to live with the tenets of literary romanticism, which rest on the foundation of philosophical romanticism; being a born romantic artist does not mean that the production of successful and critically accepted romantic literature is going to come easily. Of course, the absolutely pure romantic artist says that he writes only to fulfill his pure self, and so what the rest of the world thinks makes no difference. Of course, no one writes books about such artists. For the individual romantic artist, the tenets of literary romanticism are as difficult to come by as they are to follow, because in truth, the individual spirit can follow no other spirit. In short, the philosophical basis of romanticism is always going to be in conflict with the facts of the world, literary and otherwise. Mansfield's own husband, a much-admired literary critic and sometime novelist, was not a romantic artist but a resident of the literary world. Regardless of how much Mansfield and Murry personally loved each other, they lived in two different worlds; their constant physical separations were but symptomatic of their spiritual separation, despite the number of times that Mansfield may have proclaimed herself and Murry to be of one mind and spirit. All other persons, in romantic theory, can only approach spiritual union with the romantic artist; the twain can never be finally joined. Murry, perhaps being more the faithful husband than sound literary critic, argues that the distinction between a romantic and a classical writer is not literary at all but philosophical and moral: "The point to be remembered is that the judgement whether a writer is Romantic or Classical is a moral judgement, undoubtedly necessary to a fundamental criticism, but out of place in a discussion of style."[1] Such assertions do absolutely no good (in fact, they may do absolute harm) in a reader's pursuit of some appreciation for and understanding of Katherine Mansfield's short stories. If we allow Murry to pass such a moral judgment on the short stories of his wife, then they will have to be found to be good stories because they take the "right" position about human relationships, because they do assert some of those final supernal truths, rather than bringing aesthetic pleasure while perhaps establishing for some readers a few tentative and temporary truths about the human condition. If we allow Murry his position, then Mansfield's best stories (why only the best ones?) can give us final answers rather than just stays against the chaos. Although the romantic writer understandably can come to feel that her answers to what life means are *the* answers, it surely must be one of the tasks of the literary critic to keep pointing out to the Mansfields, Wordsworths, and Keats of this world that no answer is *the* answer but that many answers may, in fact, be answers.

As Mansfield (the artist and the woman) speaks to us from her *Journal*, her *Scrapbook*, and her letters, we will hear her struggling with the fact that a born romantic artist must exist in many worlds other than the "natural" one of her soul, nature, and her art. I have organized Mansfield's expressions of herself and her stated feelings about these other worlds into five categories: writing, life, love, nature, and the real self. The quotations from Mansfield's writings are used to demonstrate the kind of person she was, how she manifested those inherent romantic and artistic qualities, and how she responded to other individuals in her life and to the human and natural worlds around her. Some connections are made between what Mansfield says in this private writing and in her correspondence and what she says in some of the short stories discussed in Part 1. This part closes with evaluations of Mansfield made by several personal acquaintances.

On Writing

Mansfield was in her seventeenth year when she wrote from London to her cousin Sylvia Payne about how her father had insisted that she drop her plans to pursue a career as a cellist: "It was a fearful disappointment—I could not tell you what I have felt like—and do now when I think of it—but I suppose it is no earthly use warring with the Inevitable—so in the future I shall give *all* my time to writing."[2] Less than two years later (4 March 1908) and back in New Zealand, she told Sylvia that "I have finished My First Book. If it never gets published— you shall laugh with me over its absurdities" (O'Sullivan, 41). One of her first expressions of her belief in the need for ongoing romantic revolts against ordinary society comes the same month in a letter to her sister Vera:

> I am ashamed of young New Zealand, but what is to be done. All the firm fat framework of their brains must be demolished before they can begin to learn. They want a purifying influence—a mad wave of pre-Raphaelitism, of super-aestheticism, should intoxicate the country. They must go to excess in the direction of culture, become almost decadent in their tendencies for a year or two and then find balance and proportion. We want two or three persons gathered together to discuss line and form and atmosphere and sit at the street corners, in the shops, in the houses, at the Teas. (O'Sullivan, 44).

Obviously, the above suggested changes in New Zealand society would take the form of a revolution rather than the kind of cure supposedly achieved through satire, a primary literary form of the classical and neoclassical writers. Although much of Mansfield's first published book of stories, *In a German Pension*, is composed of satire, she knew that such was not her "natural" tone of voice. Writing in her *Journal* on 4 April 1914, she expressed her feelings about the "lonely," "hideous" day she had. She wrote: "Nothing that isn't satirical is really true for me to write just now. If I try to find things lovely, I turn pretty-pretty. And at the same time I am so frightened of writing mockery for satire that my pen hovers and won't settle."[3]

The struggle to find and hold onto what Mansfield would have thought of (sometimes, at least) as her "true" voice continued even after she "fell into the open arms of" "The Aloe," on 24 March 1915, as cited in Part 1. Not quite two years later, writing on 22 January 1916, Mansfield asked herself questions about her writing and expressed the real concern that she might have found so much happiness in her life and in being in love that she had lost her need to express herself through short stories:

> Now, really, what is it that I do want to write? I ask myself, Am I less of a writer than I used to be? Is the need to write less urgent? Does it still seem as natural to me to seek that form of expression? Has speech fulfilled it? Do I ask anything more than to relate, to remember, to assure myself?
>
> There are times when these thoughts half-frighten me and very nearly convince. I say: You are now so fulfilled in your own being, in being alive, in living, in aspiring towards a greater sense of life and a deeper loving, the other thing has gone out of you.
>
> But no, at bottom I am not convinced, for at bottom never has my desire been so ardent. Only the form that I would choose has changed utterly. I feel no longer concerned with the same appearance of things. The people who lived or whom I wished to bring into my stories don't interest me any more. The plots of my stories leave me perfectly cold. Granted that these people exist and all the differences, complexities and resolutions are true to them—why should *I* write about them? They are not near me. All the false threads that bound me to them are cut away quite.
>
> Now—now I want to write recollections of my own country. Yes, I want to write about my own country till I simply exhaust my store. Not only because it is "a sacred debt" that I pay to my country because my brother and I were born there, but also because in my thoughts I range with him over all the remembered places. I am never far away from them. I long to renew them in writing. (*Journal*, 93–94)

It is important to note that Mansfield expresses concern that the relatively happy life she was then living and the love that she was enjoying might be factors in keeping her from writing, thereby indicating one of the constant dangers to the romantic writer: Some of the things of this world may actually become good enough to replace the pursuit of the ideal, which ideally ought to take place through art and not through life and love, because life and love, no matter how good and self-satisfying they may be, can never hope to attain the levels of "truth" and "beauty" that can be attained only through a work of art, such as a Grecian urn or a poem about one.

Mansfield not only wrestled with questions concerning what people she should write about in order to achieve the truths she wished to set forth in short stories, but she also worried about both the shortness of the form and the haste of a story to complete itself, both factors keeping her from telling what she knew:

> Tchehov [Chekhov] made a mistake in thinking that if he had had more time he would have written more fully, described the rain, and the midwife and the doctor having tea. The truth is one can get only *so much* into a story; there is always a sacrifice. One has to leave out what one knows and longs to use. Why? I haven't any idea, but there it is. It's always a kind of race to get in as much as one can before it *disappears*.
>
> But time is not really in it. Yet wait. I do not understand even now. I am pursued by time myself. The only occasion when I ever felt at leisure was while writing "The Daughters of the Late Colonel." And at the end I was so terribly unhappy that I wrote it as fast as possible for fear of dying before the story was sent. I should like to prove this, to work at *real leisure*. Only thus can it be done. (*Journal*, 287)

Talk of muses that descend and stories that seem to have lives of their own implies that a romantic writer like Mansfield lacks control of what she is doing. But Mansfield could be concerned with technique. Following an otherwise unpublished passage in her *Journal* about the Sheridans of "The Garden Party" and "The Doll's House," she wrote this analysis:

> (But this [the passage] is not expanded enough, or rich enough. I think still a description of the hour and place should come first. And the light should fall on the figure of Mrs. S. on her way home. Really I can allow myself to write a great deal—to describe it all—the baths, the avenue, the people in the gardens, the Chinaman under the tree in May Street. But in that case she won't be conscious of these things. That's bad. They must be seen and felt by her as she wanders home. . . . That sense of flowing in and out of houses—going and returning—like the tide. To go and not to return. How terrible! The father in his dressing-room—the familiar talk. His using her

hair-brush—his passion for things that *wear well*. The children sitting round the table—the light outside, the silver. Her feeling as she sees them all gathered together—her longing for them always to be *there*. Yes, I'm getting nearer all this. . . .) (*Journal*, 324–25)

In short, what the writer does with the real objects of the real world in moving them into the art object is what makes all the difference in the world.

On Life

The ambiguous relationships that exist between life and art are probably a greater burden to the romantic writer than any other kind of writer because she has simultaneously to find art in life and life in art. There is no way to back off and take an objective look at either; neither is separable from the other or from the artist. Mansfield revealed how she struggled with these ambiguities in trying to fulfill, only eight months before her death, a request from Clement Shorter for a twelve-part serial for publication in *Sphere*. Mansfield's six stories previously published there led to some strong criticism at the time and to Alpers's conclusion that these stories "did lasting damage to her reputation." Although Alpers characterizes these stories as being "some more of those clever stories of 'English' couples toying with love,"[4] the fact is that two of the six are from memories of Mansfield's childhood in New Zealand—"Her First Ball" and "The Voyage." Of the remaining four, I have discussed "Mr. and Mrs. Dove," "An Ideal Family," and "Marriage à la Mode" at length in Part 1, attempting to demonstrate that they do have some qualities in themselves and some significance in the Mansfield canon. What is more important now, however, is that Mansfield's words in the *Journal* about how best to fulfill her obligation to Shorter for the serial brought the writer face to face with the issues of which "life" to transform into art and how to do it:

> I thought of the Burnells, but no, I don't think so. Much better, the Sheridans, the three girls and the brother and the Father and Mother and so on, ending with a long description of Meg's wedding to Keith Fenwick. Well, there's the first flown out of the nest. The sisters Bead, who come to stay. . . . [my ellipsis] Yes, I've got the details all right. But the point is—Where shall I begin? One certainly wants to dash.
>
> Meg was playing. I don't think I ought to begin with that. It seems to me the mother's coming home ought to be the first chapter. The other can come later. And in that playing chapter what I want to stress chiefly is: Which is the real life—that or this?—late

afternoon, these thoughts—the garden—the beauty—how all things pass—and how the end seems to come so soon.

And then again there is the darling bird—I've always loved birds—Where is the little chap? . . .

What is it that stirs one so? What is this seeking—so joyful—ah, so gentle! And there seems to be a moment when all is to be discovered. Yes, that is the feeling. . . .

The queer thing is I only remember how much I have forgotten when I hear that piano. The garden of the Casino, the blue pansies. But oh, how *am* I going to write this story? (*Journal*, 313–14)

What Mansfield started writing is "The Doves' Nest," one of fifteen incomplete stories printed in *The Short Stories of Katherine Mansfield*. And what is particularly interesting is that it is not about either the Burnells or the Sheridans and is not set in New Zealand but, rather, is about the Fawcetts and is set on the Riviera. Although the *Journal* entry quoted above indicates that Mansfield once intended to use her New Zealand life for this story and realized that she had to choose between the fictional Burnells and the fictional Sheridans—both of which are surrogates for her own Beauchamp family—she must have had so much trouble at this late point in her life getting her art back to the life of New Zealand that she was forced to take the shorter route to her lives in England and France. That at this point in her artistic life she had in her memory not only the real Beauchamps but also, for her, the almost-real Burnells and Sheridans must have been a strong inhibiting factor to her creativity, as if her physical condition were not sufficient detriment. The real life she had lived as Kass Beauchamp was now so confused with the two fictional lives she had created for Kezia Burnell and Laura Sheridan that Mansfield had trouble distinguishing life from art in order to use life to create more art. But such seems to be the quandary that the romantic artist who lives life for art and creates art from her life is likely to find herself in from time to time.

Although Mansfield regularly held up "life" for examination in both personal and fictional writing, the closer she got to death, the more she seemed to question what it means "to live," to seek out what life is or, better, what it can be. In the following words she recalled her "first conversation," on 30 August 1922, with A. R. Orage, editor of *New Age* when Mansfield first broke into professional print in 1910 and now an evangelist for the Gurdjieff Institute, where Mansfield hoped to find her pure personal and spiritual life at last:

> On that occasion I began by telling him how dissatisfied I was with the idea that Life must be a lesser thing than we were capable of "imagining" it to be. I had the feeling that the same thing happened to nearly everybody whom I knew and whom I did not know. No sooner was their youth, with little force and impetus characteristic of youth, done, than they stopped growing. At the very moment that one felt that now was the time to gather oneself together, to use one's whole strength, to take control, to be an adult, in fact, they seemed content to swop [*sic*] the darling wish of their hearts for innumerable little wishes. Or the image that suggested itself to me was that of a river flowing away in countless little trickles over a dark swamp.
>
> They deceived themselves, of course. They called this trickling away—greater tolerance—wider interests—a sense of proportion—so that work did not rule out the possibility of "life." Or they called it an escape from all this mind-probing and self-consciousness—a simpler and therefore a better way of life. But sooner or later, in literature at any rate, there sounded an undertone of deep regret. There was an uneasiness, a sense of frustration. One heard, one thought one heard, the cry that began to echo in one's own being: "I have missed it. I have given up. This is not what I want. If this is all, then Life is not worth living."
>
> But I *know* it is not all. How does one know that? Let me take the case of K. M. She has led, ever since she can remember, a very typically false life. Yet, through it all, there have been moments, instants, gleams, when she has felt the possibility of something quite other. (*Journal*, 329–30)

Perhaps, for example, while writing, or maybe even rereading, the final lines of "The Garden Party" or "The Doll's House."

On Love

If the confrontation of the facts of everyday life, the quotidian, by a
sensitive soul who has not lost the imaginative capabilities of youth
represented for Mansfield the highest form of life in both fact and fiction, then the communion of two such souls represented the highest
form of love. The difficulties in attaining to such a love in a "world
that is too much with us,"[5] even between two persons who "loved"
each other as much as John Murry and Katherine Mansfield did, are
made manifest in the following passage from the *Journal* entry of 15
December 1919:

> After a few days J.'s letters in response to *my* depressed letters began
> to arrive. There were a series of them. As I grew depressed, *he* grew
> depressed, but not for me. He began to write (1) about the suffering
> I caused him; *his* suffering, *his* nerves, *he* wasn't made of whipcord
> or steel, the fruit was bitter for *him*. (2) a constant cry about money.
> He had none; he saw no chance of getting any—"heavy debts"—
> "as you know I am a bankrupt." "I know it sounds callous." "I can't
> face it." These letters, especially the letters about money, cut like
> a knife through something that had grown up between us. They
> changed the situation for me, at least, for ever. We had been for two
> years drifting into a relationship, different to anything I had ever
> known. We'd been *children* to each other, openly confessed children,
> telling each other everything, each depending equally upon the
> other. Before that I had been the man and he had been the woman
> and he had been called upon to make no real efforts. He'd never
> really "supported" me. When we first met, in fact, it was I who kept
> him, and afterwards we'd always acted (more or less) like men-
> friends. Then this illness—getting worse, and turning me into a
> woman and asking him to put himself away and to *bear* things for
> me. He stood it marvellously. It helped very much because it was a
> romantic disease (his love of a "romantic appearance" is *immensely*
> real) and also being "children" together gave us a practically unlim-
> ited chance to play at life, not to live. It was child love. Yes, I think
> the most marvellous, the most radiant love that this world knows:
> terribly rare. We've had it. But we were not *pure*. If we had been,

he'd have faced coming away with me. And that he could not do. He'd not have said he was too tired to earn enough to keep us here. He always refused to face what it meant—living alone together for two years on not much money. He said and three-quarters of him believed: I couldn't stand the strain of it with you ill. But it was a lie and a confession that all was not well between us. And I always knew it. Nevertheless, I played up, and truly even in October I clung to him still—still the child—seeing as our salvation a house in the country, in England, *not later than next May* and then never to be apart again. The letters—ended all of it. *Was* it the letters? I must not forget something else.

All these two years I have been obsessed by the fear of death. This grew and grew and grew *gigantic*, and this it was that made me cling so, I think. Ten days ago it went, I care no more. It leaves me perfectly cold. Well it was that *and* the letters perhaps. Gone is my childish love—gone is my desire to live in England. I don't particularly want to live with him. (*Journal*, 183–84)

Although Mansfield clearly assigns most of the blame for the death of their ideal love to Murry's self-centeredness and his inability to keep the world of money out of their relationship, surely we must see that her assumption that the strong man is supposed to support the weak woman smacks of those old traditional values of her parents' generation. Children are not "naturally" affected by male and female values and responsibilities. Those things come with children's natural fall into sexuality and their indoctrination into social practices. The kind of love for which Mansfield yearned can rarely exist in this childlike way among adults, especially if one of those adults insists on being a "woman" and making her mate a "man" in the primary senses that those words have carried throughout Judeo-Christian history. Mansfield recounts at least one time when she did feel a communion of spirits with a man and without the relationship's becoming sexual. Although the close feeling she proclaims between herself and Scottish painter J. D. Fergusson surely must have rested in part on the exchange of adult and artistic ideas, her description makes it sound like a meeting of kindred spirits that might take place at any age:

I came home this afternoon and Fergusson came in. I was standing in the studio, someone whistled on the path. It was he. I went out and bought some milk and honey and Veda bread. By and by we sat down and had tea and talk. This man is in many ways extraordinarily like me. I like him so much; I feel so *honest* with him that it's simply one of my real joys, one of the real joys of my life, to have him come and talk and be with me. I did not realise, until he was here and we ate together, how much I cared for him—and how much I was really at home with him. A real understanding. We might have spoken a different language—returned from a far country. I just felt all was well, and we understood each other. Just that. And there was "ease" between us. There is a division: people who are my people, people who are not my people. He is mine. I gave him for a pledge my little puddock [a brass frog of which she was particularly fond]. (*Journal*, 123–24)

Obviously, William Wordsworth was also one of Mansfield's "people" and not just because they shared an attitude toward nature and the artist's creative relationship with it. She also believed that Wordsworth and his sister Dorothy enjoyed a relationship similar to what Mansfield yearned for with Murry and what she may have hoped to attain with her brother before his death. It should be noted that under the usual circumstances the sister-brother relationship exists without the threat of sex. The following is Mansfield's quotation from William Knight's introduction to *Dorothy Wordsworth's Journal*, a quotation that gains significance from Mansfield's emphatic rejoinder to Knight: "'All the Journals contain numerous trivial details, which bear ample witness to the "plain living and high thinking" of the Wordsworth household—and, in this edition, samples of those details are given—but there is no need to record all the cases in which the sister wrote, "To-day I mended William's shirts," or "William gathered sticks," or "I went in search of eggs," etc. etc.' There is! Fool!" (*Journal*, 210). Mansfield thus proclaims vigorously the importance of such "trivial details" to both the artist who would write and the man and woman who would proclaim their loving relationship by happily sharing such daily chores. Mansfield did not believe that she was ever in such a relationship for any period of time.

On Nature

Mansfield's love of and attitude toward nature is exceedingly Wordsworthian: "By health I mean the power to live a full, adult, living, breathing life in close contact with what I love—the earth and the wonders thereof—the sea—the sun. All that we mean when we speak of the external world. I want to enter into it, to be part of it, to live in it, to learn from it, to lose all that is superficial and acquired in me and to become a conscious direct human being" (*Journal*, 333). This desire, expressed in the final year of her life, does not differ greatly from Mansfield's lifelong attitude toward nature. In 1920 she quoted Samuel Taylor Coleridge from his *Table Talk*: "I, for one, do not call the sod under my feet my country. But language, religion, laws, government, blood—identity in these makes men of one country," to which Mansfield responded, "The sod under my feet makes *mine*" (*Journal*, 222).

Mansfield's expression of her particular feelings on 5 January 1915 sounds the note that so regularly appears in her *Journal* about the human truths that can grow out of the beauties of the natural world and our acceptance of our necessary work, our "trivial details" within it that help keep us a part of nature: "Saw the sun rise. A lovely apricot sky with flames in it and then a solemn pink. Heavens, how beautiful! I heard a knocking, and went downstairs. It was Benny cutting away the ivy. Over the path lay the fallen nests—wisps of hay and feather. He looked like an ivy bush himself. I made early tea and carried it up to J., who lay half awake with crinkled eyes. I feel so full of love to-day after having seen the sun rise" (*Journal*, 65).

One last quotation about Mansfield's use of highly emotional experiences connects her again to the great romantic poet Wordsworth and his famous dictum that poetry is the "spontaneous overflow of powerful feelings" that has its origin in "emotion recollected in tranquility."[6] In a 1916 letter to Bertrand Russell, after saying "I dont [*sic*] in the least know definitely *how* to live," Mansfield first lists a long series of experiences in nature that brought her beauty and pleasure and then concludes about these experiences:

All this—and all this is nothing—for there is so much more. When I am overcome by one of the fits of despair all this is ashes—and so intolerably bitter that I feel it never can be sweet again—But it is— To air oneself among these things, to seek them, to explore them and then to go apart and detach oneself from them—and to write— after the ferment has quite subsided—

After all youll [*sic*] cry me very vague & dismiss me perhaps as a woman with an ill regulated mind. (O'Sullivan, 287–88)

Mansfield was a Wordsworthian romantic artist who found more truth and beauty in the production of art than in the direct experience of life and nature, no matter how emotionally satisfying those experiences occasionally were in themselves or how necessary to the production of art.

On the Real Self

Even if Mansfield were born with those tendencies, talents, and emotions that her readers can generally assign to the romantic artist she was still an individual who had to reckon with the possibility or probability that she had a real self, a core of being, within her more discernible general nature. Whatever affinities she may have had with her romantic predecessors, she was not William Wordsworth or John Keats. Of course, Mansfield did not solve the riddle or get out of the maze of what it means to be true to oneself, although in a long passage called *The Flowering of the Self* she certainly takes to task all those persons of her own or any generation who so willingly rest their case on Polonius's glib words of advice to Laertes about being true to himself. Mansfield wrote:

> When autograph albums were the fashion—sumptuous volumes bound in soft leather, and pages so delicately tinted that each tender sentiment had its own sunset sky to faint, to die upon—the popularity of that most sly, ambiguous, difficult piece of advice: "To thine own self be true" was the despair of collectors. How dull it was, how boring, to have the same thing written six times over! And then, even if it was Shakespeare, that didn't prevent it—oh, *l'âge d'innocence!* from being dreadfully obvious. Of course, it followed as the night the day that if one was true to oneself . . . True to oneself! which self? Which of many—well really, that's what it looks like coming to—hundreds of selves? For what with complexes and repressions and reactions and vibrations and reflections, there are moments when I feel I am nothing but the small clerk of some hotel without a proprietor, who has all his work cut out to enter the names and hand the keys to the wilful guests.
>
> Nevertheless, there are signs that we are intent as never before on trying to puzzle out, to live by, our own particular self. [my ellipsis] . . . free, disentangled, single. Is it not possible that the rage for confession, autobiography, especially for memories of earliest childhood, is explained by our persistent yet mysterious belief in a self which is continuous and permanent; which untouched by all we acquire and all we shed, pushes a green spear through the dead

leaves and through the mould, thrusts a scaled bud through years of darkness until, one day, the light discovers it and shakes the flower free and—we are alive—we are flowering for our moment upon the earth? This is the moment which, after all, we live for,—the moment of direct feeling when we are most ourselves and least personal. (*Journal*, 205)

Mansfield believed that only as a writer could she be most completely herself and at the same time gain a perspective of impersonality wherein she could be herself looking at herself, simultaneously praising and questioning, loving and looking askance at the persons in her life and the characters in her fiction. Only through fiction could she attain a degree of honesty about herself and the people in her life that would allow her to tell the kind of truth she speaks of in this 1919 passage: "At the end *truth* is the only thing *worth having:* it's more thrilling than love, more joyful and more passionate. It simply *cannot* fail. All else fails. I, at any rate, give the remainder of my life to it and it alone" (*Journal*, 185). Of course, like all of us who make vows and resolutions to let our better self (the real one, of course) control our weaker selves, Katherine Mansfield had trouble keeping this one.

Personal Responses of Her Friends

Even if Katherine Mansfield had a single self, there were also by necessity multiple public selves to which many persons who knew Mansfield have responded. Other than her husband, the person who spent the most time with the adult Mansfield was Ida Baker, renamed during their student days at Queen's College as Lesley Moore and regularly called LM by Mansfield and many others. In fact, Ida Baker's memories of her life, written when she was in her eighties, is entitled *Katherine Mansfield: The Memories of LM*. The following summary of how LM viewed KM is extracted from the epilogue to this book (all ellipses are mine in the remainder of this part):

> There was a bell-like quality in her rich low voice and her singing was a high, pure soprano; she was neither tall nor short but so well-proportioned that one did not notice; she had a sensitive, finely curved mouth and deep, dark, steady eyes that really *looked*: but above all she was herself, clear-cut and individual. In gaiety and joy or in despair, whether in life or in her stories, she was always Katherine.
>
> She was a born actress and mimic, and even in her ordinary everyday life took colour from the company she was in. I think this was what puzzled people. She would give apparently all of herself to a situation or a person as they demanded, and then, if anything came too close, particularly when she had become ill and frail, she would withdraw into her remoteness, only to change colour again to meet some fresh contingency. . . .
>
> Fastidious in her personal possessions, Katherine had a great love of order, and by striving for just the right material or colour or arrangement she could impart a little of her own personality to the simplest and most modest surroundings. Even a temporary resting-place would take on an atmosphere of "home."
>
> Brave and adventurous through her many adversities, it was only in the early years that Katherine ran away from the quick-sands of her own inexperience; and then not through fear but to escape to firm ground where, safe from the stress and entanglement of life, she could sit quietly and write the record of it. Paper and pencil were

to be her sword and shield: she was upheld continuously by the guiding thought of her work. . . .

In our friendship there was complete honouring of individual independence. Her life was vivid, aware, strong; she was always the instigator, consciously choosing and directing her life, down to the smallest detail. . . .

There is one thing that I cannot stress too strongly, as it runs all through Katherine's life and in many ways explains her relationships with people. She always gave fully and generously of herself to all who were lucky enough to make contact; the relationship, as long as it existed, was intensely alive. But she herself stood apart.

. . . One other thing needs explanation, if only because people have so often angered me by saying, "She must have been a very difficult person to live with." Most of the belittling remarks Katherine made about me, generally in illness, and mostly from her letters to Murry which he published, were just a freeing of herself from some momentary vexation. As expressed in Katherine's words, however, they sounded worse—and I surely must have vexed her often. Katherine's so-called rages, due to frustration—the breaking point of her tolerance under stress of constant pain.

But at other times Katherine's complaints were deliberately made, and I knew it, to give Murry just the kind of self-support that his character needed, an assurance that he was the first, the all-important, the master in the sometimes difficult intimacies of three.[7]

Literary historian and critic Frank Swinnerton wrote about Mansfield in two separate surveys of the literary scene of which she was a part. In his earlier book he describes his first meeting with Mansfield, in 1912:

I found myself enchanted by a small, very slim, very dark girl who spoke in a carefully modulated murmur, hardly parting her lips, as if she hummed or intoned her words. She sat very still, smiling faintly, and explained in this low voice, with much sweetness, that she did not know quite what she should do in the future—with her life, she meant, for the alternatives of children, literature, and career seemed all to be possible. . . . The beautiful idol-like quietness of Katherine Mansfield made a great impression upon me then, as it always did—she was one of the most enchanting young women I had ever met. . . .

Katherine Mansfield was a very fastidious person, a literary person, enamoured of Art. She was herself a simple person. But she tried hard, at one time or another, to be something a little more grandiose. Any reader of her letters will be struck by occasional notes of exclamatory and italicized sentiment, and by her flutterings after fundamental critical conclusions; at times I think she was a little too literary and perhaps even a little insincere—both accidents inevitable in one who was quickly moved by her own writings and by kindness from others, and one who was still, as far as I can see, vainly seeking some convincing aesthetic touchstone.[8]

Writing some fourteen years later, Swinnerton, in comparing Mansfield and her cousin and fellow author Elizabeth Russell, seems to stress Mansfield's childlike qualities: "Nobody knew what passed in Katherine's mind. It was egocentric; and it had two chief preoccupations, Art and her own unmatured childishness. . . . Katherine's mind remained unaffected by her experience. She never grew up. She pretended a great deal to herself, especially about Art. She was prevented by ineradicable conventionality from being whole-heartedly bohemian."[9]

Another literary figure who described his first meeting with Mansfield is Sidney Schiff, who wrote under the pseudonym of Stephen Hudson. Their first meeting took place in late 1920 or early 1921, although the article from which the following quotations come was not published until 1958:

> Her voice was soft, low, a little hoarse. Her elocution extremely clear. . . . [S]he was frail to see. Frail and brilliant eyes, hair, skin. Dainty, fresh and elegant, when she laughed, radiant.
>
> She was waiting within the shelter of the glazed portico, dressed with fastidious elegance. She followed the fashion but interpreted it inconspicuously to suit her taste. In the sunshine, she looked still more fragile than indoors. Her skin was too transparent, her colour too hectic, her eyes too bright for placid health. Delicate but not ill, not even threatened with illness.
>
> Nothing escaped her eye and vivid comment. . . .
>
> I opened a bottle of champagne for lunch and the meal became a lively feast. Katherine's laughter was tuneful and infectious. Every turn of the conversation disclosed mutual sympathies and aversions. Though her spontaneous desire was to please, she was anything but complaisant in her comments and criticism of people and things. She gave herself up to the moment almost with abandonment, talked with light and easy grace and when Violet [Schiff's wife] reticent of speech, expressed an opinion, listened with concentrated attention.

Later in the article, Schiff (the article is under Hudson's name) describes a subsequent visit to Mansfield's apartment at Mentone, France:

> She had the faculty of imparting elegance to the most commonplace surroundings. A few trifles, sofa cushions, a vase of flowers were the only visual emblems of this subtle emanation which was nevertheless pervasive. I found her reclining on a sofa near the window opening on to a small neglected garden full of flowers, looking delicate and pale through the rosy flush of her cheeks. She had heightened the redness of her lips discreetly, her eyes were very bright. Her self-adornment was personal and restrained yet agreeably noticeable; it showed that she attached importance to her appearance and knew her seductiveness was increased rather than diminished by her disease. [10]

Virginia Woolf, who had helped publish *Prelude* in 1918 and who had an off-and-on, sometimes competitive and jealous relationship with Mansfield, wrote in her diary entry of 31 May 1920 about their first meeting in eight months, because of Mansfield's being out of London over the winter:

> I had my interview with KM. on Friday. A steady discomposing formality & coldness at first. Enquiries about house & so on. No pleasure or excitement at seeing me. It struck me that she is of the cat kind: alien, composed, always solitary & observant. And then we talked about solitude, & I found her expressing my feelings, as I never heard them expressed. Whereupon we fell into step, & as usual, talked as easily as though 8 months were minutes. A queer effect she produces of someone apart, entirely self-centered; altogether concentrated upon her "art": almost fierce to me about it, I pretending I couldn't write. [Mansfield said,] "What else is there to do? We have got to do it. Life—" then how she tells herself stories at night about all the lives in a town. "Its a spring night. I go down to the docks—I hear travellers say—" acting it in her usual way, & improvising. [11]

Highly emotional events of the 1919–1920 winter spent first in Ospedaletti, Italy, and then in Menton brought Mansfield into a new state of mind that she characterizes in her *Journal* as knowing that she must pass "from personal love which has failed me to greater love. I must

give to the whole of life what I gave to him [Murry]" (228). Virginia
Woolf records how she observed this change in Mansfield during lunch
on 5 June 1920:

> I lunched with K.M. & had 2 hours priceless talk—priceless in the
> sense that to no one else can I talk in the same disembodied way
> about writing; without altering my thought more than I alter it in
> writing here. . . . We talked about books, writing of course: . . .
> Then I said "You've changed. Got through something"; indeed
> theres [*sic*] a sort of self command about her as if having mastered
> something subterfuges were no longer so necessary. She told me of
> her terrific experiences last winter—experiences of loneliness
> chiefly; alone (or only with "Leslie Moor" alias Ida Baker) in a stone
> house with caverns beneath it into which the sea rushed; how she
> lay in bed alone all day with a pistol by her; & men banged at the
> door. (Woolf, 45)

Another commentator on Mansfield, one with whom she and Murry
had a long and tumultuous relationship, was D. H. Lawrence. In a
November 1913 letter to Murry, Lawrence gives him advice on how to
handle Mansfield, advice that reflects not only Lawrence's highly idiosyncratic view of all male-female relationships but his reading of what
Mansfield wanted from her relationship with Murry, some five years
prior to their marriage:

> When you say you won't take Katherine's money, it means you don't
> trust her love for you: When you say she needs little luxuries, and
> you couldn't bear to deprive her of them, it means you don't respect
> either yourself or her sufficiently to do it. . . .
>
> If you work yourself sterile to get her chocolates, she will most
> justly detest you—she is *perfectly* right. . . . She doesn't want you to
> sacrifice yourself to her, you fool.
>
> If you want things to come right—if you are ill, and exhausted,
> then take her money to the last penny, and let her do her own house-
> work. Then she'll know you love her. You can't blame her if she's
> not satisfied with you. [12]

Lawrence, whose "habit of taking his friends and acquaintances as
models for his fictional characters"[13] may be compared with Mansfield's own habit, used Mansfield as a model for Gudrun Brangwen in

Women in Love, although, as Richard Aldington also says in his introduction to the novel, "we should hardly recognise Gudrun as Katherine
Mansfield if it had not been officially given out" (Aldington, xi). Although the following description of Gudrun may suggest some of
Mansfield's qualities, there may be more interest in comparing the second paragraph quoted below—about Gudrun's experience with the
poor—and Mansfield's portrayal of Laura Sheridan's experience in
"The Garden Party." At any rate, here is Lawrence's first descriptive
passage about Gudrun, age twenty-five, the same age as Mansfield in
1913 when Lawrence started his novel:

> Both [Gudrun and her sister Ursula, who was based on Frieda Law-
> rence] had the remote, virgin look of modern girls, sisters of Artemis
> rather than of Hebe. Gudrun was very beautiful, passive, soft-
> skinned, soft-limbed. She wore a dress of dark-blue silky stuff, with
> ruches of blue and green linen lace in the neck and sleeves; and she
> had emerald-green stockings. Her look of confidence and diffidence
> contrasted with Ursula's sensitive expectancy. the provincial people,
> intimidated by Gudrun's perfect sang-froid and exclusive bareness
> of manner, said of her: "She is a smart woman."[14]

The sisters are walking through a coal-mining area, being stared at by
poor women with their "arms folded over their coarse aprons":

> Gudrun went on her way half dazed. If this were human life, if these
> were human beings, living in a complete world, then what was her
> own world, outside? She was aware of her grass-green stockings, her
> large grass-green velour hat, her full soft coat, of a strong blue colour.
> And she felt as if she were treading in the air, quite unstable, her
> heart was contracted, as if at any minute she might be precipitated
> to the ground. She was afraid.
>   She clung to Ursula, who, through long usage, was inured to this
> violation of a dark, uncreated hostile world. But all the time her
> heart was crying, as if in the midst of some ordeal: "I want to go
> back, I want to go away, I want not to know it, not to know that this
> exists." Yet she must go forward. (Lawrence, 6)

Another fictional portrait of Mansfield, although probably not as fictional as Lawrence's, was written by William Orton, a schoolteacher
with whom Mansfield had a strong emotional, though probably not

sexual, affair beginning in 1910 (Alpers, 117). Michael in the following passage is Orton himself in his heavily autobiographical novel *The Last Romantic*:

Catherine—Katharina she called herself (she was being very Russian just then)—had published one or two pieces in the *New Age*, which were shortly afterwards collected as her first book; and Orage had also taken a small essay of Michael's. But it was at the Berlings' they met in Hampstead, playing tennis. A sort of instant recognition passed between them, and going home in the momentary silence of a tube station, Catherine suddenly said, "Do you believe in Pan?" . . . [Two nights later in her flat] She had made the place look quite beautiful—a couple of candles stuck in a skull, another between the high windows, a lamp on the floor shining through yellow chrysanthemums, and herself accurately in the centre, in a patterned pink kimono and white flowered frock, the one cluster of primary brightness in the room. . . . "Young," noted Michael, "with an inviolable virginity, whom more than life can offer were needed to satisfy, for whom not love itself could bring the balm of quiescence." Which was good enough as far as it went; but it left out the central fact because there was never anything to be written about that—the fact that they had this other world in common, and that it was a happy one. More than happy, it was secure: "Catherine and I," said Michael, "are stronger than anything that can happen to us."

. . . It was literally true of Catherine at this time (she and Michael were twenty-one when they met) that she lived to write. She was writing a good deal of poetry, partly under the influence of Walt Whitman; but all her writing was a kind of poetry, not so much in respect to form or content as in its extreme intensity and accuracy of realization. And now that she was sure she could write—for Orage's recognition, to everybody who knew him, was about as final a verdict as one could get—life was fundamentally good and secure, whatever kind of life it might be. More consistently than Michael, she remained the artist, subject always to art's pitiless demand for purity, clarity, and thoroughness; but so long as she obeyed that—and she could not disobey—she was happy.

The business of living under such conditions needs careful management; but Catherine, conscious (or subconscious) of her New Zealand background, chose to think she was tough and could play fast and loose with it. The collapse of her marriage had done far more harm than she or anyone else realized; for at heart she was idealistic and deeply religious. But she was also one of the few people in whom the "thirst for experience" is a genuine thing, indicating a genuine need.[15]

Direct statements made by John Murry about Katherine Mansfield are so readily available that it seems to make more sense in closing this section to bring together excerpts from their letters to each other on 4 and 8 December 1919. These letters may show Mansfield and Murry at their worst with each other. From this exchange and from their subsequently being physically together over the Christmas of 1919 developed the major change in Mansfield that Virginia Woolf could see in her face the following summer. Besides, the composite portrait drawn of Mansfield through this exchange of letters complements and reinforces the portraits drawn above. The letters back and forth between Mansfield and Murry during the fall and early winter of 1919 were increasingly full of complaints and self-justifications, not all of which can be laid to their long-term conflicts, his insecurities, and her illness. Mansfield knew of Murry's involvements with Dorothy Brett and Elizabeth Bibesco (Alpers, 317, 323) when she wrote as follows to Murry on 4 December 1919:

> If I can be sure of getting better—absolutely sure—would you mind very much if I adopted a child? Evidently on the cards I may have to spend a good deal of my life—alone—and I can't stick it. I think, I'm sure in fact, I could manage as regards money, and I want to adopt a baby boy of about *one* if I can get him. I cannot do it if you dislike the idea, because of course he would be always with us when we were together just like our own child—and you might hate that.
>
> On the other hand, when I am alone, he'd keep me from utter loneliness and writing these agonizing letters!! I thought I'd ask Brett to be his guardian supposing anything were to happen to me.

Mansfield continued writing that same day, after receiving two letters from Murry, one "telling me of your cold." Of her move from Ospedaletti to Menton and of her state of mind, she wrote:

> I am sure Menton will do wonders for my old depression. I've great hopes of it. Bogey, forgive me, all you tell me about the house—I can't help feeling it's all part of a hideous vile joke that's being played on us for les autres to read about in days to come. I *can't* see it except like this. I sometimes even get to the pitch of believing

that subconsciously you are aware of this, too, and with colossal artistry are piling on delicate agony after delicate agony—so that *when*
the joke is explained, all will be quite perfect,—even to a silver tea-
pot for her.

Mansfield then followed with a poem of seven stanzas, of which this
is the first one:

The New Husband

Someone came to me and said
Forget, forget that you've been wed.
Who's your man to leave you be
Ill and cold in a far country?
Who's the husband—who's the stone
Could leave a child like you alone?[16]

Murry, of course, responded immediately:

This morning [8 December] I got your Thursday letter & the verses
called "The New Husband." I've wired to you to-day to say I'm
coming out for Christmas. I feel there's not much I can say.

I don't think that at any time I've had a bigger blow than that
letter & those verses. Even now they hardly seem like a letter &
verses—more like a snake with a terrible sting. But it's kind of you
to tell me you have those feelings: far better, for me anyhow, than
keeping them from me. You have too great a burden to bear; you
can't carry it. Whether I can manage mine, I don't know. We'll see
when I get out to you.

What is certain is that this can't go on—something must change.
What can go on—I don't know yet. . . .

If I felt certain that my being there would really make things right
until May, then nothing would matter. But now I can't pretend to a
certainty I don't feel. We'll just have to leave it & see. Anyhow, I
just couldn't go on with the A[*thenaeum* editorial work] if you were
to go on feeling like this. I'm absolutely incapable of work, now.
That sounds, and is, selfish. But you have told the truth; & I must
tell the truth. I'm not made of steel, myself. And it's becoming a
great effort to do what I have to do sanely—do you think I can do
anything with this [last four lines of the stanza quoted above] ringing
in my ears. There's nothing to say to that. All that I implore you is
to say what you want. That will help.

No, no, no—all this is too *hard*. I don't mean it—something dif-

ferent. But I must keep sane. I'm coming quickly, darling—then
we'll see, we'll see.[17]

Mansfield wrote as follows on the back of the envelope: "This letter
killed the Mouse, made the Worm creep underground and banished
the Dream Child for ever. Before I had received it I had learned to live
for Love and *by* Love. I had given myself up—and a kind of third
creature *US* was what I lived by. After I had read it, quite apart from
me, my own self returned *and* all my horror of death vanished. From
this date I simply *don't care* about death! No question of heroics—or
life not being worth living or anything like it. I simply feel alone again.
Voilà" (Murry, 241).

Notes to Part 2

1. J. Middleton Murry, *The Problem of Style* (London: Oxford University Press, 1930), 146.

2. Vincent O'Sullivan and Margaret Scott, eds., *The Collected Letters of Katherine Mansfield*, vol. 1 (Oxford, Oxford University Press, 1984), 18. Hereafter cited in text as O'Sullivan.

3. *Journal of Katherine Mansfield*, "Definitive Edition," ed. J. Middleton Murry (London: Constable & Co., 1954), 58–59. Hereafter cited in text as *Journal*.

4. Antony Alpers, *The Life of Katherine Mansfield* (New York: Viking Press, 1980), 338. Hereafter cited in text as Alpers.

5. The opening words of one of Wordsworth's best-known sonnets.

6. From the preface to *Lyrical Ballads*, 1802.

7. Lesley Moore (née Ida Baker), *Katherine Mansfield: The Memories of LM* (London: Michael Joseph, 1971), 233–36.

8. Frank Swinnerton, *The Georgian Literary Scene, 1910–1935* (London: Hutchinson & Co., 1950): 203–6.

9. Frank Swinnerton, *Figures in the Foreground: Literary Reminiscences, 1917–1940* (Garden City, N.Y.: Doubleday & Co., 1964), 59–60.

10. Stephen Hudson, "First Meetings with Katherine Mansfield," *The Cornhill Magazine*, no. 1017 (Autumn 1958): 203–8.

11. Virginia Woolf, *The Diary of Virginia Woolf*, ed. Anne Oliver Bell (New York: Harcourt Brace Jovanovich, 1978), 43–44. Hereafter cited in text as Woolf.

12. D. H. Lawrence, *The Letters of D. H. Lawrence*, ed. James T. Boulton (Cambridge: Cambridge University Press, 1981), 110–11.

13. Richard Aldington, introduction to *Women in Love*, by D. H. Lawrence (New York: Viking Press, 1968), xi.

14. D. H. Lawrence, *Women in Love* (New York: Viking Press, 1968. Hereafter cited in text as Lawrence.

15. William Orton, *The Last Romantic* (New York: Farrar & Rinehart, 1937), 269–70, 274–75.

16. Katherine Mansfield, *Katherine Mansfield's Letters to John Middleton Murry: 1913–1922*, ed. John Middleton Murry (New York: Knopf, 1951), 425–27.

17. John Middleton Murry, *The Letters of John Middleton Murry to Katherine Mansfield*, ed. C. A. Hankin (New York: Franklin Watts, 1983), 239–40. Hereafter cited in text as Murry.

Part 3

THE CRITICS

Introduction

Any sample of the critical, analytical, and appreciative writing about an author and an author's work ought to demonstrate what a complete reading of that material will reveal: that the best writers can be approached from many directions, that the works can be studied from many angles, that there is no "right" reading of a given short story, and that indeed differences of judgment and interpretation are the norm rather than the exception. Unfortunately, many younger students of literature go looking for that nonexistent "right" answer in order to flatter a teacher, and many experienced readers assert that they have found the definitive reading in order to flatter themselves.

In choosing the following excerpts, I have had to omit many equally perceptive articles. Since my primary purpose is to introduce the general reader and the beginning student to the criticism of Mansfield's work, rather than to demonstrate the full extent and quality of that criticism, I can only hope that the disservice done by this act of omission is as forgivable as my acts of commission in violating the unity and organicism of essays that deserve better. The Bibliography should help satisfy critical appetites that have merely been whetted by these selections.

The excerpts from six long essays reprinted in this part were chosen for a number of reasons and are placed in the order in which I state those reasons. First, I wanted to show what other writers of fiction think about their fellow artist, and so I chose sections from a collection of the essays of Willa Cather, an American, and from the introduction to a collection of Mansfield's short stories by Elizabeth Bowen, a Britisher. Next, I wanted to demonstrate how other critics make generalizations about works and how they support those generalizations through references to particular stories, thus the portions of essays by George Shelton Hubbell on Mansfield's attitude toward and treatment of children and by Cherry Hankin on Mansfield's handling of the ends of her stories. It also seemed appropriate to choose material from a critic whose total work places Mansfield in perspective with other writers; accordingly, the excerpts from Andrew Gurr's book *Writers in Exile:*

Part 3

The Identity of Home in Modern Literature show the effect on Mansfield of living primarily in an alien land. Gurr, in the whole text, compares and contrasts these effects on Mansfield and five other writers: V. S. Naipaul, Ngugi wa Thiong'o, Jean Rhys, Doris Lessing, and Patrick White. Literary scholarship, too, needs to be recognized and demonstrated, although I have had to omit the heart of how Philip Waldron supports his contention that John Middleton Murry put together a supposedly unified and organic Mansfield *Journal* out of bits and pieces of disparate material that his wife left him. The seventh item here is a complete essay of close textual analysis, chosen because it is about one of Mansfield's most controversial stories, "Bliss," and because it is a model of analytical criticism on a single story. I think that Helen Nebeker's essay is well done and thorough, and I am convinced of the truth of her reading.

In reproducing the material from these sources, I have left them as they were originally printed, with the exception of dropping the name *Katherine* or *Miss* from in front of *Mansfield*, fixing some titles, and moving some punctuation and quotation marks around to continue patterns used elsewhere in this book. I have also changed all page references to the stories to coincide with those in *The Short Stories of Katherine Mansfield* when the original authors did not cite that text. All ellipses in Part 3 are mine.

Although it pains me greatly to let Cather continue to call Mansfield "first-rate" because as a writer Mansfield shares "his timbre, something "that is his very own," perhaps by leaving Cather's text unchanged I can remind contemporary readers of those linguistic bad habits that were once so much a part of our language that even a woman writing about a woman could not escape the masculinization of her prose.

Willa Cather

Every writer and critic of discernment who looked into Katherine Mansfield's first volume of short stories must have felt that here was a very individual talent. At this particular time [1936] few writers care much about their medium except as a means for expressing ideas. But in Mansfield one recognized virtuosity, a love for the medium she had chosen.

The qualities of a second-rate writer can easily be defined, but a first-rate writer can only be experienced. It is just the thing in him which escapes analysis that makes him first-rate. One can catalogue all the qualities that he shares with other writers, but the thing that is his very own, his timbre, this cannot be defined or explained any more than the quality of a beautiful speaking voice can be.

It was usually Mansfield's way to approach the major forces of life through comparatively trivial incidents. She chose a small reflector to throw a luminous streak out into the shadowy realm of personal relationships. I feel that personal relationships, especially the uncatalogued ones, the seemingly unimportant ones, interested her most. To my thinking, she never measured herself up so fully as in the two remarkable stories about an English family in New Zealand, "Prelude" and "At the Bay."

I doubt whether any contemporary writer has made one feel more keenly the many kinds of personal relations which exist in an everyday "happy family" who are merely going on living their daily lives, with no crises or shocks or bewildering complications to try them. Yet every individual in that household (even the children) is clinging passionately to his individual soul, is in terror of losing it in the general family flavour. As in most families, the mere struggle to have anything of one's own, to be one's self at all, creates an element of strain which keeps everybody almost at the breaking-point.

. . . In those simple relationships of loving husband and wife, affectionate sisters, children and grandmother there are innumerable shades of sweetness and anguish which make up the pattern of our lives day by day, though they are not down in the list of subjects from which the conventional novelist works.

Mansfield's peculiar gift lay in her interpretation of these secret accords and antipathies which lie hidden under our everyday behaviour, and which more than any outward events make our lives happy or unhappy. Had she lived, her development would have gone on in this direction more than in any other. When she touches this New Zealand family and those far-away memories ever so lightly, as in "The Doll's House," there is a magic one does not find in the other stories, fine as some of them are. With this theme the very letters on the page become alive. She communicates vastly more than she actually writes. One goes back and runs through the pages to find the text which made one know certain things about Linda or Burnell or Beryl, and the text is not there—but something was there, all the same—is there, though no typesetter will ever set it. It is this overtone, which is too fine for the printing press and comes through without it, that makes one know that this writer had some of the gift which is one of the rarest things in writing, and quite the most precious.

Elizabeth Bowen

How good is Katherine Mansfield's character-drawing? I have heard this named as her weak point. I feel one cannot insist enough upon what she instinctively grasped—that the short story, by reason of its aesthetics, is not and is not intended to be the medium either for exploration or long-term development of character. Character cannot be more than *shown*—it is there for use, the use is dramatic. Foreshortening is not only unavoidable, it is right. And with Mansfield there was another factor—her "stranger" outlook on so much of society. I revert to the restrictedness of her life in England, the eclecticism of her personal circle. She saw few people, saw them sometimes too often. This

Excerpted from *Stories by Katherine Mansfield*, selected and with an introduction by Elizabeth Bowen (New York: Random House, 1956), v–xxiv. © 1956 by Alfred A. Knopf, Inc. Reprinted by permission of Alfred A. Knopf, Inc.

could account for her tendency to repeat certain types of character. This restless New Zealand woman writing of London deals with what was more than half a synthetic world: its denizens *are* types, and they remain so—to the impoverishment of the London stories. The divorce of the intelligentsia from real life tends to be with her an obsessive subject—aggravated more than she knew, perhaps, by her sense of being far from her home base. Her sophisticates are cut out sharply, with satire; they are animated, expressive but two-dimensional.

In the South of France stories, characters are subsidiary to their environment; they drift like semi-transparent fish through the brilliantly lighted colours of an aquarium. Here, Mansfield's lovely crystallization of place and hour steals attention away from men and women. Could *she* not bear to examine these winter visitors—idle, half-hearted and non-indigenous? Tense Anglo-Saxons, they contrast with physically equable busy natives—beauty cheats them, Nature withholds her secret. Patient is the husband without a temperament; true is Miss Brill to her fur necktie; the young girl is a marvel of young hauteur. Yet these three, even, no more than brush one's memory: the South of France stories are about moods.

Mansfield, we notice, seldom outlines and never dissects a character: instead, she causes the person to expose himself—and devastating may be the effect. The author's nominal impassivity is telling. I should not in the main call her a kind writer, though so often she is a pitiful one. Wholly benevolent are her comedies: high spirits, good humour no less than exquisite funniness endear to us "The Daughters of the Late Colonel," "The Doves' Nest," "The Singing Lesson." Nor is the laugh ever against a daydreamer.

The New Zealand characters are on a quite other, supreme level. They lack no dimension. Their living-and-breathing reality at once astonishes and calms us: they belong to life, not in any book—they existed before stories began. In their company we are no longer in Mansfield's; we forget her as she forgot herself. The Burnells of *Prelude*, "At the Bay," and "The Doll's House" are a dynasty. Related, though showing no too striking family likeness, are the conversational Sheridans of "The Garden-Party." Of Burnell stock, graver and simplified, are elderly Mr. and Mrs. Hammond of "The Stranger"—and Mansfield's equivalent of James Joyce's "The Dead." Alike in Burnells, Sheridans, and Hammonds we feel the almost mystic family integration. Husbands and fathers are convincing; men give off an imposing masculinity. These men, women, old women, young girls, children are in a major key. I do not claim that the New Zealand stories vindicate Mansfield's character-drawing—the *drawing* is not (to my mind) elsewhere at fault. What she fails at in the European stories is full, adult character-*realization*—or, should one say, materialization? Her Londoners are guessed at, her New Zealanders known. As to the Burnells she had information of the kind not gained by conscious experience. Writing of these people, she dwells upon them—her art grew not only from memory but from longing.

The New Zealand stories are timeless. Do the rest of the Mansfield's stories "date"? I find there is some impression that they do—an impression not, I think, very closely checked on. To an extent, her work shows the intellectual imprint of her day, many of whose theories, tenets, preoccupations seem now faded. It is the more nearly *mondaine*, the "cleverer" of her stories which wear least well. Her psychology may seem naive and at times shallow—after all, she *was* young; but apart from that much water has flowed under bridges in thirty years. "Bliss," "Psychology" and *Je ne parle pas français* (technically one of her masterpieces) give out a faintly untrue ring. And one effect of her writing has told against her: it was her fate to set up a fashion in hypersensitivity, in vibratingness: it is her work in this vein which has been most heavily imitated, and travesties curdle one's feeling for the original. . . .

She wrote few love stories; those she did today seem distant, dissatisfying. Staking her life on love, she was least happy (I think) with love in fiction. Her passionate faith shows elsewhere. *Finesses*, subtleties, restless analysis, cerebral wary guardedness hallmark the Mansfield lovers. Was this, perhaps, how it was in London, or is this how Londoners' *amours* struck [a young New Zealand girl used to] beaux, waltzes, muslin, moonlight, murmuring sea?

George Shelton Hubbell

Samuel Butler held that children are human beings, and Katherine Mansfield insists upon treating them as such; notwithstanding our ancient social usage to the contrary. Time was when "John Smith and family" would satisfactorily designate a whole household. Nowadays, "Mr. and Mrs. John Smith and family" will generally do. But in the Mansfield stories each child must be treated separately, and the parents are lucky if they get as much attention as their offspring, or as much respect.

This super-inclusive democracy may seem strange to some readers, but the acceptance of it is not without rewards. Those who have fallen into the habit of looking upon the child's world as a mistake, to be corrected by experience and education, need to learn how many of the solid values of life we adults are missing. When Mr. Burnell goes to work, and when Mrs. Burnell sits down to imagine vain things, little Kezia Burnell walks forth to her life in the garden or by the shore. To stodgy grownups who know what to expect from book-keeping and from house-keeping, this fresh child-life is a revelation.

But Kezia, the essential child, is very near the essence of all life—that fugitive lifeness, which generally evades expression. Mansfield somehow manages to catch the very soul of it in a subtle net of narrative. The little girl's words have been weighed and tested; and only those are set down which are at once typically human and unmistakably Kezia. Trees, bushes, and flowers are seen from her height, and all objects or people are considered from her point of view; while we are with her in the story, the world that we see is her world. Our perception is quickened to the clearness of her keen child-senses; we interpret everything through her child-mind, free, unsuspicious, unafraid, winged by imagination. And yet we stand aside and see her too; though the sight is quite ordinary as compared to our exhilarating participation in her living consciousness. . . .

Sometimes Mansfield seems to slip herself and her readers in among a group of children, taking on the spirit of their thoughts, without adapting the story to the mind of any particular child. A happy instance

Excerpted from "Katherine Mansfield and Kezia," *Sewanee Review* 35, no. 3 (July 1927) : 325–35. Reprinted by permission of the editors of the *Sewanee Review*.

of this is the play of the two youngsters in "See-Saw." Everything harmonizes so well with their scale that we seem to be one with them. We fit in as the little lamp fitted the doll's house. . . .

But our understanding of Kezia is far more personal and intimate than [what we feel about the children in "See-Saw"]. And her adventures, though simple enough, are broadly human, of the utmost significance. In "The Little Girl," which is the history of her relations with her father, we follow her through the same gropings that exercised the ancient Hebrews in the Old Testament, as they strove to straighten out their religious ideas. It is not without significance that they, too, finished by considering Jehovah as a Father. The saddest part of Kezia's experience was the spanking, but she came through it bravely; even Job could hardly boast a sweeter spirit in affliction. . . . Job's problem has not yet been satisfactorily settled. Neither has Kezia's [in asking "What did Jesus make fathers for?"]. . . .

In *Prelude* we get the very best about Kezia. In the moving day adventure which she and Lottie had with the rude little Samuel Josephs, we see the pride and courage of the child, which is the essence of human heroism. We smile at it, but our mirth is perverse. The seeds of tragedy are there. For all heroism is proud, selfish, deluded, as well as heroic. . . . I suspect that, for better or for worse, Kezia came naturally by her heroism.

[Kezia escapes from her sister Isabel's manipulations by going "just away."] And to what tremendous advantage she went away! To our advantage as readers, that is; for Mansfield somehow got into her mind . . . and stayed there for two and half pages almost without a break. It is marvelously fascinating, as we are permitted to think the child's thoughts there in the garden. The words themselves are not hers—the author has helped her to them, as it were—but the selection of objects for emphasis, the point of view, the train of ideas, the emotional reactions—all are Kezia's. . . . Kezia will never be a reformer; but she has the making of a first-class philanthropist, if her naivete could be depended upon to last.

That, however, is the very thing which most certainly will not last. The elements of sophistication and the roots of sin are plainly to be discerned in the experiences of Kezia. The most memorable of such experiences was the beheading of the duck [in *Prelude*]. . . . You may be sure that she never forgot, never recovered, never felt quite the same again. . . .

[Many other children in Mansfield's stories appear as] little heads that lift themselves in the most unexpected places and then disappear forever. But, one and all, they are so vivid and life-like that they remain indelible in the memory. . . . [Passages about them] would make in themselves a remarkable commentary upon the art of the writer, upon the understanding of childhood.

But after all, the essence of the matter is to be found in Kezia. She is the complete child, having whom, we may take the others for granted. And in her, and in the art by which she is presented, we find the best possible summary of the genius of Katherine Mansfield.

Cherry Hankin

Because Katherine Mansfield's influence on the development of the modern short story in English was a formative one, an examination of the means she used to bring her stories to the point of closure is instructive; it furthers our understanding of the short story form itself, as well as of her own artistic practice.

Now one of the most striking features which emerges from a close study of Mansfield's stories is the frequency with which some pattern involving fantasy informs her "sense of an ending." . . . [The human propensity to dream about alternatives] and a concomitant sharp contrast between fantasy and reality . . . set in motion the change, if not the reversal of expectations, that characterizes the conclusions of a great many of Mansfield's stories. Indeed, in terms of their endings, her stories may be grouped roughly into four different categories: the central character may experience a reversal of expectations and disillusionment; an impending disillusionment or change in expectations may be deflected by the central character's transmutation of the experience into something positive; a reversal or surprise occurs—but at the expense of the reader rather than the character; or the ending may involve a surprise which is merely clever and effects no change in the attitude of either the central character or the reader. What is significant

Excerpted from "Fantasy and the Sense of an Ending in the Work of Katherine Mansfield," *Modern Fiction Studies* 24, no. 3 (Autumn 1978) : 465–74. © 1978 by Purdue Research Foundation, West Lafayette, Indiana. Reprinted by permission.

is that the stories acknowledged to be among Mansfield's best fall into the first two categories. In these stories, which almost invariably involve a reversal of expectations, fantasy plays a prominent role in the denouement. On the other hand, there is markedly less employment of fantasy in the endings of the generally weaker stories which fall into the last two categories.

Clearly, it is not just the element of fantasy in a central character's thought processes which sets apart . . . often-discussed works from Mansfield's less popular stories. But what does occur in the denouement of these stories . . . is a dreaming about alternatives and a reversal of expectations which emotionally engages the reader as well as the central character. Mansfield's gift, in her finest writing, is an ability to focus upon a situation in which the illusions and fantasies of her fictional characters echo those of ordinary human beings. Her appeal is not merely to the reader's sympathies; it is to his instinctive recognition of the similarly competing hopes and fears in his own inner life.

[This essay examines four early stories (1903–1909) to show that] . . . the conclusions of even Mansfield's immature stories demonstrate her inherent sense of the dramatic, her concern to ring down the curtain convincingly, and so complete the design. . . .

Mansfield continued to write about the conflict between fantasy and reality until the end of her life; and I would venture to suggest that it was because this subject sprang directly from her own earliest and deepest imaginative experiences that she was able to portray it with such emotional conviction. To survey some of her best-known stories is to observe not only her increasingly sophisticated treatment of the theme, but also the extent to which the contrast between illusion and disillusion shaped the endings of her mature narratives and, indeed, their form. When one considers the preoccupations of her adolescent writing, it is perhaps not surprising that the stories which engage the reader's emotions most immediately conclude with the disillusionment or defeat which is concomitant with a movement from fantasy to reality. A variation of this characteristic ending occurs when a character averts disillusionment by reversing the movement and recovering, or gaining sudden access to, the world of dream. In both types of narrative the outcome is aesthetically satisfying; there is a sense in which the artistic pattern is rounded off and the laws of life, like the laws of fiction, are felt to be obeyed.

[An analysis of the endings of eight of the major stories leads to the conclusion that] . . . Mansfield brought to her subject an acute psychological perceptiveness and an instinctive sense of form. There is a conclusiveness and a finality about the ends of her best stories which make us accept the aesthetic as well as the emotional rightness of the experience we have just sustained.

Andrew Gurr

Katherine Mansfield wrote a number of fine, delicate stories about the relationship between Murry and herself and about their English life. To the insect-on-a-pin scrutiny of the triangle, her French lover Francis Carco, Murry and herself in "Je parle pas français" of February 1918 she added the portrait of the man living abroad for the sake of his invalid wife in "The Man without a Temperament" in January 1920. The period in 1917 when the two of them had separate establishments lies behind "Psychology," while "The Escape" (1920) is a superb portrait of a strained, destructive relationship, the woman as compulsive bitch and the man as tortured evader. . . . To these stories of strain she added others from her English experience, catching moments of infidelity, epiphanies of English life ("Bliss," "Revelations"). Others were written with the same incisive anger that informs the earlier stories she wrote for *The New Age.* There is a surge of feminism behind "The Little Governess" (1915) and "Mr. Reginald Peacock's Day" (1917), and a warmer kind of derision in the stories of human weakness such as "Marriage à la Mode" or the extended joke "Feuille d'Album." Taken as a whole, however, they vary in quality much more than the New Zealand stories. One of the English stories in particular may help to explain why.

All the English or European stories share the economic precision of phrase which is one of the characteristics of her style. The last section of "Life of Ma Parker," for instance, opens with a pair of similes which compose a marvellously exact and compact word-picture: "It was cold in the street. There was a wind like ice. People went flitting by, very

Excerpted from *Writers in Exile: The Identity of Home in Modern Literature*: (Atlantic Highlands, N.J.: Humanities Press, 1981), 41–44. © 1981 by The Harvester Press, Hempstead, England. Reprinted by permission.

fast; the men walked like scissors; the women trod like cats." The short sentences hurry along with the urgent rhythm of the street scene. The strong evocative similes make the atmosphere thus created visual. And the similes do not stand out as a casual vividness. The mature stories are all perfectly integrated structures—difficult to quote from without the feeling that the passage has been crudely ripped out of its context. In this passage, for instance, the men like scissors and the women like cats are at the same time visual images and menacing ideas, the dangerous hostile creatures of the chilly world Ma Parker walks out into. In fact the paragraph continues directly from the similes into Ma Parker's response to the cold world of scissors and cats: ". . . And nobody knew—nobody cared. Even if she broke down, if at last, after all these years, she were to cry, she'd find herself in the lock-up as like as not." A superb pair of similes, deployed with an exact regard for their place in the story as a whole. And yet this paragraph, the opening of the final section of "Life of Ma Parker," is to my mind one of the most awkward passages in all of Mansfield's mature writing. It is bad for reasons which I think relate directly to her position as an exile in the England of which she is writing. Integrated though the similes are into the associative design of the whole, their evocativeness has to appear as Ma Parker's own verbalisation of her grief. And it does not work. The vision—scissors and cats in the cold street—is Ma Parker's but the words are the author's. Ma Parker is too alien, too different a creature from her author to share her language. The technique of sliding from an authorial voice imperceptibly into the mind of the beholder was a normal device in Mansfield's short stories, one of the advances she made for the short story form. In the opening [paragraph] of "At the Bay" it works immaculately. . . . The morning landscape and mood are evoked by a seamless transition from word-painting to the child's vision from her bedroom overlooking the bay. No such seamless transition is possible with Ma Parker because to her author she is an alien.

The story of Ma Parker is of course a rather special case in the Mansfield canon. Interior monologue was by no means an essential technique, and some of the best of the English stories do very well without it. And yet the best of the English stories are the ones which venture the shortest distance from her own intimate experience: "The Man without a Temperament," "The Daughters of the Late Colonel," "Bliss." The finest of them all, "The Daughters of the Late Colonel," was readily recognised and acknowledged by its model Ida Baker as [a kind caricature of herself and Mansfield's cousin Sylvia Payne]. It was actually written in Ida's company, and Ida made the tea for a celebration when it was finished. Apart from that one rather anomalous achievement, Mansfield wrote her best about intimately known subjects held at a distance. "The Man without a Temperament" and "Je ne parle pas français" she wrote while she was in France and Murry was in London. England was too oppressive, her isolation from it was never sufficiently complete for the elevation and detachment in which she wrote at her best. The isolation she needed was a freedom from the social pressures which the metropolis laid on her. Even Murry became oppressive in time.

Philip Waldron

The first edition of Katherine Mansfield's *Journal* was published in 1927 with John Middleton Murry as editor. In 1939 Murry supplemented this material with the *Scrapbook* and in 1954 we received what Murry called the "definitive edition" of the *Journal*. The final edition was definitive because it incorporated passages from the 1939 *Scrapbook*, some previously unpublished material, and contained various minor corrections. The careful reader of Murry's brief preface can however see a certain amount of contradiction in his description of what is involved. On the one hand he speaks of the *Journal* as though such a thing existed distinct from a mass of miscellaneous material. Thus he writes: "passages have been incorporated which, though actually published in the *Scrapbook* in 1939, really belong to the *Journal* and would have been included in it, if they had been discovered in time." On the other hand Murry says that the material of which the *Journal* is composed "is of various kinds: comments, confessions, and unposted letters, which she had the habit of writing in the same exercise books as those in which she wrote her stories; fragmentary diaries . . . brief and often difficult notes for the stories; marginal comments in the books she read." It is far from clear what could dis-

Excerpted from "Katherine Mansfield's Journal," *Twentieth-Century Literature* 20, no. 1 (January 1974): 11–18. Reprinted by permission.

tinguish such miscellanea from "scrapbook" material. Murry goes on to strengthen the feeling that he has edited a journal, not created a book from stray oddments, by writing that "what has survived is, almost wholly, that which, for one reason and another, she wished to survive." The implication is that she had conceived the material in book form and contemplated the publication of it.

It was impossible to study the MSS until the Government of New Zealand bought from Murry's estate in 1958 the material from which the *Journal* was edited, and deposited it in the Alexander Turnbull Library, Wellington. Professor I. A. Gordon gave a brief and general but excellent description of the Mansfield papers in the New Zealand periodical *Landfall* in 1959. Nothing else has been published on this material and it is the aim of this article to give a clearer and more detailed account of the contrast between the published *Journal* and the material from which it was fashioned.

The material consists of four diaries which, like most diaries, are copious in early January but quickly peter out; some thirty notebooks and exercise books; and several hundred loose sheets of paper. There is no evidence whatsoever that Mansfield ever had publication in mind. In fact the flyleaf of the 1915 Diary is inscribed: "I shall be obliged if the contents of this book are regarded as my private property." Apart from the general point Murry makes about the *Journal* being an arrangement of confessional, creative, or autobiographical oddments into a cohesive book by the editor, the published *Journal* differs from the original MSS in a number of ways. These include the arbitrary and usually unnoted omission of material which Murry thought to be of less interest; the omission of what is illegible or difficult to read; the omission or toning down of passages which could embarrass or offend people who knew Mansfield (including the editor); the omission or toning down of material which would reflect Mansfield's tetchy, even bitchy personality or her less conventional sexual proclivities; arbitrary dating and arrangement of passages; and general stylistic tidying up of the material (often in fact to the literary detriment of that material). Besides these conscious alterations to the text, a general and extreme carelessness affects the text of almost every page.

[Numerous comparisons between MSS material and Murry's edited books lead to the conclusion that] it would be unrealistic to claim that the intrinsic literary interest of Mansfield's *Journal* were other than minor. But it is the central document of the life, mind, and emotions of a still very interesting short story writer. The distortion of the text by Murry has in turn distorted the personality of the writer herself as we know it, and is to some extent responsible even now for the myth still current in France of a temperamentally ethereal figure. Mansfield's *Journal* could never again arouse the interest it commanded in the years when it was something of a best seller, and I cannot see that a more adequate edition would result in a radical revision of her status.

Helen Nebeker

In analyzing Katherine Mansfield's short story "Bliss," critics, although aware of its importance, have generally failed to grasp fully the significance of the central symbol, the pear tree, with its implications for the character of Bertha. In so doing, they have overlooked the covert sexual nuances of the story.

The overt sexual nuances are, of course, undeniable. In the first scene—each section of the story is essentially a dramatic scene viewed through the mind of Bertha—Bertha's feeling of "bliss" burns in her bosom and causes her to wonder why one has a body if it has to be "shut up in a case like a rare, rare fiddle" (338). In contradiction, her frigidity is revealed in the images of cold—the room which is chilly, the cold air on her arms, the cold mirror which reflects a seemingly vibrant woman. Further emphasizing her frigidity is her inability to bear the constricting clasp of her coat another moment. A few lines later, Bertha's revulsion toward the sexual is implicit in her reaction to the grey cat "dragging its belly," followed by the black one. This revulsion is again emphasized in the last scene as Bertha sees Eddie "following [Pearl] like the black cat following the grey" (350). The sensuality of Harry who glories in his "'shameless passion for the white flesh of the lobster' and 'the green of pistachio ices'" (345) escapes no one. And even the phallic overtones of the pear tree, as Bertha and Pearl view it together, have been pointed out. However, the full sexual

From "The Pear Tree: Sexual Implications in Katherine Mansfield's "Bliss," *Modern Fiction Studies* 18, no. 4 (Winter 1972) : 545–51. © 1972 by Purdue Research Foundation, West Lafayette, Indiana. Reprinted by permission.

implications inherent in the pear tree image have never been pursued. For it is not until one understands the botanical significance of the pear tree that they can be perceived.

When we first see the pear tree, through Bertha's eyes, it stands at the far end of the garden, "slender . . . in fullest, richest bloom . . . perfect as though becalmed . . . it had not a single bud or a faded petal" (341). To Bertha, "the lovely pear tree" is "a symbol of her own life" (342), perfect complete. But ironically, Bertha does not realize even as she dresses in imitation of the tree, even as the story ends, how valid her comparison has been.

Because the pear tree is by nature bi-sexual, its "perfect flowers" contain both male and female organs of propagation (that is the sense of "perfect" botanically). Sometimes in such bi-sexual trees, a condition occurs wherein the anther (male organ) ripens before the stigma matures enough to receive the pollen, and, hence, self-fertilization cannot occur. Furthermore, such flowers often cannot even be cross-pollinated; hence no fertilization is possible. Thus a pear tree in perfect bloom may be sterile, unable to bear fruit, without "a single bud or a faded petal." Even as it symbolizes perfection, it is in essence incomplete, beautiful but non-functional.

That this concept of the *sterility* of the pear tree—rather than its flowering as postulated by most critics—is what Mansfield had in mind seems obvious when we note that juxtaposed with our first view of it is an immediate contrast in fertility, "the red and yellow tulips, heavy with flowers" (341); the two cats, sexual, fecund—the grey cat obviously heavy with life. Bertha, drawn by the virginal quality of the tree, turns away from these evidences of bursting life with a shiver, only to be overcome by the cloying smell of the jonquils.

If we pursue the idea of the bi-sexual, flowering but not fruitful pear tree, a first reaction of a reader may be to insist that the unfruitful image is not relevant to Bertha. Bertha Young, at the age of thirty (which incidentally is not young at all in child-bearing terms), has a child and hence has realized fruit. But if we analyze Bertha's relationship with her daughter, an irrefutable fact emerges through the essentially third person limited point of view which Mansfield employs. Although Bertha seems to resent Nanny's possessiveness toward Little B, "watching them . . . like the poor little girl in front of the rich little girl with the doll" (339), she, a thirty-year-old matron, makes little effort to assert her authority. Rather she begs, as would a child or an immature young person in the face of authority, "Oh, Nanny, do let me finish giving her her supper while you put the bath things away" (339). Nanny acquiesces reluctantly and Bertha, having fed her "little precious," murmurs "You're nice—you're very nice! . . . I'm fond of you. I like you" (340). Then she further reassures herself of her feelings—as she will do repeatedly throughout the story concerning other aspects of her life—thinking, "indeed, she loved Little B so much— her neck as she bent forward, her exquisite toes as they shone transparent in the firelight . . ." (340). The point here is that Bertha does not see Little B (note the indication that the baby is only a reflection of herself) in any normal terms of mother love. The child is not her care, her creation, the fruit of her womb; rather she is a "doll," an exquisite art treasure to be appreciated aesthetically much as the fruit arranged in a glass bowl on a blue dish has been admired in the previous scene. Bertha, in a very real sense, has not produced fruit, only a flower. This analogy extends itself in the pear tree, for only the mature, slow-growing tree bears fruit; the immature yields blossoms.

Now the question of the more difficult but intriguing question of the bi-sexuality of the tree image and its application to Bertha remains to be clarified. Perhaps the easiest way to develop this issue is by analyzing the consecutive development of the various womb-phallus symbols. These begin in the first scene when Bertha arranges the fruit. Inasmuch as a woman usually arranges flowers for a party, the choice of fruit for this scene in itself assumes sexual significance. Furthermore, while the fruits mentioned are all round—with the significant exception of the pear, which is both round (ovate) and elongated— Bertha arranges them in "two pyramids of . . . bright, round shapes" (338–39). This curious womb-phallic[1] image will be re-evoked later in the scene where Bertha and Pearl stand looking at the "slender, flowering tree" which seems "like the flame of a candle, to stretch up, to point, to quiver in the bright air, to grow taller and taller . . . almost to touch the rim of the round, silver moon" (347). In both of these instances we perceive, then, the two sexual images, male and female united and the bi-sexual implications are clear.

Furthermore, these bi-sexual nuances are also sustained by the color imagery of the fruits. There are white grapes covered with a silver bloom; Bertha will later don a white dress while Pearl will appear "all in silver." Also significant here is a big cluster of purple grapes which Bertha "had bought to tone in with the new dining-room carpet." It was "absurd," but she had thought, "I must have some purple ones to bring the carpet up to the table" (338). Curiously enough, the white flower of the pear tree has a purple anther (the organ containing the pollen for fertilization). Again the sexual implications are evident. Bertha, overcome by rising, subconscious desire, at once drawn to and repulsed by the sexual, acts out this subliminal frustration artistically and visually.

Subsequent to this scene where Bertha arranges the fruit, Mansfield lays her groundwork for disclosing Bertha's latent homosexuality. We discover, as Bertha prepares for her party, that among her guests will be Pearl Fulton. Pearl is a "find of Bertha's. . . . They had met at the club and Bertha had fallen in love with her, as she always did fall in love with beautiful women who had something strange about them" (340–41). Certainly here the homosexual overtones are inescapable. We are clearly told that Pearl is not the first woman of her type whom Bertha has cultivated, and this point is further emphasized when Pearl finally arrives; Bertha smiles "with that little air of proprietorship that she always assumed while her women finds were new and mysterious" (344). The reader knows, moreover, that Bertha has literally thrust Pearl upon Harry. Her motivation in this can only be conjectured. While she subconsciously seeks out those women who complement her own nature, does she coincidentally, and still subconsciously, procure for Harry those "strange," "cool," passionate women of "white flesh" with the veiled "eyelids of Egyptian dancers" and thus, as he eventually seduces them, derive a vicarious sensual experience such as she fears in the reality? Certainly, in view of such lines as, "Why doth the bridegroom tarry?" (344) and "She [Bertha] . . . positively forgot until he had come in . . . that Pearl Fulton had not turned up" (344) and "they waited . . . just a trifle too much at their ease, a trifle too unaware" (344), we would be fools to assume that similar episodes have not occurred previously. Furthermore, when Pearl comes in all in silver and Bertha, taking her arm to lead her into the room, discovers that the cool arm starts "blazing—blazing—the fire of bliss that Bertha did not know what to do with" (344), we would be more than blind if we failed to realize that it is Pearl who stirs Bertha, that it is she who has been the focus of Bertha's thoughts, not Harry.

Bertha herself is, of course, totally unaware of these undercurrents within and, at least for a time, quite honestly believes that her growing desire is for Harry. But the facts of the story deny this. Bertha sees Pearl not as one woman usually sees another but as a lover sees his love: ". . . her heavy eye lids lay upon her eyes and the strange half smile came and went upon her lips. . . . Bertha knew, suddenly, as if the longest, most intimate look had passed between them . . . that Pearl Fulton . . . was feeling just what she was feeling" (345). A few lines later as everything seems so "good," so "right," filling "her brimming cup of bliss," Bertha thinks of the pear tree, which

> would be silver now . . . silver as Miss Fulton,[2] who sat there turning a tangerine in her slender fingers that were so pale a light seemed to come from them.
>
> What she simply couldn't make out—what was miraculous—was how she should have guessed Miss Fulton's mood so exactly and so instantly. . . .
>
> "I believe this does happen, very, very rarely between women. Never between men . . . perhaps she will give a sign." What she meant by that she did not know, and what would happen after that she could not imagine. (346)

Of course, she does not know, and she cannot imagine. Conventional Bertha Young, cold, innocent wife, cannot possibly comprehend the forces tearing at her in the shape of Pearl. But caught up in the intensity of her emotions, when Pearl does give the sign, Bertha moves with her to the windows, and we see the flowering tree for the second time. No longer becalmed, no longer chaste and white, it seems to flame, to stretch, to quiver, to almost touch the round, silver moon.[3]

"How long did they stand there? Both, as it were, caught in that circle of unearthly light, understanding each other perfectly, creatures of another world. . . . For ever—for a moment? And did Miss Fulton murmur: 'Yes, Just *that*.' Or did Bertha dream it?" (347).

Now contrary to critical pronouncements on this point, we have absolutely no way of knowing what Pearl Fulton derives from this experience. We do not even know that she murmured, "Yes, Just *that*," for Bertha wonders if she had dreamed it. Since all events in this story are narratively focused through Bertha, we can only know that *she* believes that she and Pearl have shared an experience of such intimacy that "blissful treasure . . . burned in their bosoms and dropped in silver flowers, from their hair and hands" (347). It is only later, as Pearl leaves after having arranged a meeting with Harry, that Bertha realizes that what they have shared has been *only* Harry, nothing more. Then Pearl, in Bertha's eyes no longer "new and mysterious" but, by implication, like all the others who have preceded her, leaves the party like the grey cat being followed by the black.

But before this final scene, Mansfield offers further proof of the true meaning of these events, for Bertha, watching Harry offer Pearl cigarettes, thinks: "Oh, Harry, don't dislike her. You are quite wrong about her. She's wonderful, wonderful. And besides, how can you feel so differently about someone who means so much to me. I shall try to tell you when we are in bed to-night what has been happening. What she and I have shared" (348). These last two lines have led critics to point out the terrible irony of Bertha's failure to perceive the truth that what she and Pearl have actually shared is Harry. But I suggest that this is an over-simplification and that there is here a triple implication based upon the exegesis already presented in this [essay]. Suppose that Bertha, in light of her subconscious feeling for Pearl and the fact that we know she has introduced other such women into her circle before and discussed them intimately with her husband, is really saying something like the following: "Oh, Harry, don't dislike *her*. You're wrong about *her*; she's not like the others, who have always succumbed to your attentions before. She's silver and pure and special, and I'm drawn to her, and she is drawn to me with none of the ugly sexual overtones that men must experience." For this is what the overwhelming emotional experience of the pear tree, with all its hidden sexual nuances, has meant to Bertha, a communion which has cemented for her that attraction which happens "very, very rarely between women. Never between men."

The lines immediately following the "what she and I have shared" reinforce this whole interpretation, for "at those last words something strange and almost terrifying darted into Bertha's mind. And this something blind and smiling whispered to her: 'Soon these people will go. The house will be quiet—quiet. The lights will be out. And you and he will be alone together in the dark room—the warm bed . . .'" (348).

Again critics, using only the first sentence of this passage, interpret this as a sign of Bertha's subconscious foreboding concerning Harry and Pearl. But taking the paragraph as a whole, something else emerges. "Those last words" so "strange and almost terrifying" also include, "I shall tell you in bed to-night what has been happening." Implied here, then, is not only naked, overt fear, at the thought of the sexual experience perhaps awaiting her in the dark room, alone with Harry, but also a flashing awareness "strange and almost terrifying" of "what has been happening," that is, of the homosexual urges within her. But Bertha cannot admit the nature of these thoughts and quickly reassures herself, with the same sense of desperation in which she has insisted on her love for her baby and her intense states of happiness and the perfection of her life, that "for the first time in her life Bertha Young desired her husband . . . ardently! ardently! The word ached in her ardent body!" (348). Are we, at this point in what has been a carefully controlled third-person-limited narrative focus, to take these words as the truth from a suddenly omniscient narrator? Or must we sense another almost hysterical attempt on the part of Bertha to avoid recognition of an untenable truth? This seems reasonable in view of the coincident insight given into the Youngs' sterile, good-pals-and-all-that type of marriage, in which, "so frank with each other," so "modern," they can discuss Bertha's sexual inadequacies and accept the fact that Harry is "different."

However, we really do not have to speculate about this point at all, because the denouement follows quickly, and Bertha's soul is bared. For in the following scene where Bertha is supposedly shocked at discovering her husband's infidelity, we see that Pearl remains the same silver image with "moonbeam fingers . . . and her sleepy smile" (349). It is Harry, the beast with nostrils quivering and lips curled back in a "hideous" grin, who assaults Bertha's sensitivity. This is Mansfield's familiar dog image,[4] which is always associated with fright and threat, never with love and assuagement. Critics have attacked the crudity of this image[5] which detracts, they say, from the effect of Bertha's emotional shock, but I believe this was exactly Mansfield's intention. For it is not the shock of Harry's involvement which is at issue, but the horror of seeing this animal being unbelievably caressed by the silvery Pearl who answers his whispered "To-morrow" with an unuttered "Yes."

That this is the shock, the grief, is further delineated when Pearl—with whom Bertha has shared that moment of silvery communion and all that it promised—pausing to say good-bye, murmurs, "Your lovely pear tree!" and then is gone "with Eddie following like the black cat following the grey cat" (350). The silvery Pearl, the moon-child, no longer strange and mysterious and pure, but like all the others whom Bertha has known, is now the grey cat "dragging its belly." The intense, blissful experience—and all that it meant and might have meant—has been hers alone. The thing that happens "very, very rarely between women" has not happened at all. And with the words of Pearl ringing in her ears, "Your lovely pear tree—pear tree—pear tree!" Bertha runs to the window to see it, like herself, lovely, full of flower, and once again still.

Part 3

Notes

1. The "rare, rare fiddle," mentioned twice by Bertha, also evokes a similar ovate-elongated image.

2. Note that Bertha never thinks of her as simply Pearl. Three times she is referred to as Pearl Fulton but some eighteen times as Miss Fulton—four of these in the single paragraph in which Pearl and Harry caress.

3. It might be significant to point out here that the "pearl" is the stone for the astrological sign of Cancer, the Moon Child, and that "Bertha" derives from an Old German term meaning "bright or shining one." Furthermore, astrologically the moon represents the feminine principle of the universe, whereas the sun (bright and shining one) represents the masculine.

4. See Celeste Wright, "Katherine Mansfield's Dog Image," *Literature and Psychology* 10 (Summer 1960) : 80–81.

5. See Sylvia Berkman, *Katherine Mansfield: A Critical Study* (New Haven: Yale University Press, 1951), 180.

Chronology

1888	Kathleen Mansfield Beauchamp born 14 October at 11 Tinakori Road, Wellington, New Zealand, the third daughter of Harold Beauchamp and Annie Dyer Beauchamp.
1895–1898	Attends the Karori village school.
1898–1899	Attends Wellington Girls' High School. In September the *High School Reporter* publishes "Enna Blake" by Kathleen Beauchamp.
1899–1902	Kathleen and her sisters attend Miss Swainson's school.
1903	Beauchamp family sails to London, where the girls enter Queen's College in the spring. Kathleen meets Ida Baker and subsequently gives Ida the name Lesley Moore, or LM.
1904–1906	*Queen's College Magazine* publishes several sketches; in 1905 Kathleen becomes head editor. Leaves Queen's College in June 1906, returning to Wellington in October.
1907	*Native Companion* of Melbourne publishes several sketches, one being "Vignettes" by K. Mansfield. Has "love affairs" with Edith Bendall and Maata Mahupuku (Martha Grace).
1908	Returns to London.
1909	Marries George Bowden on 2 March and leaves him that evening. Travels with Garnet Trowell and becomes pregnant. Goes to Bavaria; has miscarriage.
1910	Returns to London and lives briefly with Bowden. *New Age* begins publishing her stories, with "The Child Who Was Tired" on 24 February. By July she is using Katherine Mansfield as her name for more than publication.
1911	Continues publication in *New Age*. In December *In a German Pension* is published and KM meets John Middleton Murry.

1912   JMM becomes KM's lodger in London and shortly her lover, at her suggestion. KM begins publishing in the journal *Rhythm*.

1913   *Rhythm* becomes *Blue Review*, which dies after three issues. KM's only story written this year is "Something Childish but Very Natural." The year ends with KM and JMM living in Paris.

1914   Back in England, KM and JMM become close to D. H. and Frieda Lawrence.

1915   Leslie (Chummie) Beauchamp arrives in England and becomes close to his sister before being killed in France on 7 October. KM has an affair with Francis Carco; begins publishing in *Signature*, started by Murry and Lawrence. She ends the year back in France.

1916   A year of several physical and emotional moves, into and out of Lawrence's life and into that of Lady Ottoline Morrell, at Garsington.

1917   Several items published in *New Age*, including "A Dill Pickle." Rewrites "The Aloe" as *Prelude* for separate publication by Leonard and Virginia Woolf. Continues her close association with the Garsington and Bloomsbury groups. In December a spot is discovered on KM's left lung.

1918   *Prelude* published in July and "Bliss" in *English Review* in August. Lives in South of France, Paris, London. Divorced by George Bowden, KM marries JMM on 3 May.

1919   JMM becomes editor of *Athenaeum*, for which KM writes poetry, under the pseudonym Elizabeth Stanley, and book reviews. Lives the last quarter of the year in Italy with LM.

1920   Lives in Menton, France, and London, writing several stories, including "The Life of Ma Parker," "The Young Girl," "The Stranger," and "The Daughters of the Late Colonel." *Bliss and Other Stories* is published in December.

1921   Living first in Menton and then in Switzerland, KM writes a number of stories, including "The Garden Party," "The Doll's House," "At the Bay," and "Marriage á la Mode."

1922   Against the strong objections of JMM but with the encouragement of LM, KM seeks a cure for tuberculosis through radiation treatments with Dr. Manoukhin in Paris. The combination physical-mystical treatments may actually have shortened her life. Later KM joins Gurdjieff's colony at Fontainebleau. *The Garden Party and Other Stories* is published in February; KM writes her final complete stories, "The Fly" and "The Canary."

1923   KM dies 9 January of a massive hemorrhage shortly after JMM arrives to be with her. Burial takes place on 12 January in Fontainebleau. Inscribed on her grave are Hotspur's words: "But I tell you, my Lord fool, Out of this nettle, danger, we pluck this flower, safety."

Bibliography

Primary Works

Story Collections

Bliss and Other Stories. London: Constable, 1920; New York: Knopf, 1921. "The Wind Blows," "The Little Governess," "Mr. Reginald Peacock's Day," "Feuille d'Album," "A Dill Pickle," "Prelude," "Bliss," "Pictures," *Je ne parle pas français*, "The Man without a Temperament," "Revelations," "The Escape," "Sun and Moon," "Psychology."

The Doves' Nest and Other Stories. London: Constable, 1923. "The Doll's House," "Taking the Veil," "The Fly," "Honeymoon," "A Cup of Tea," "The Canary."

The Garden Party and Other Stories. London: Constable, 1922; New York: Knopf, 1922. "Bank Holiday," "The Young Girl," "Miss Brill," "The Lady's Maid," "The Stranger," "The Life of Ma Parker," "The Daughters of the Late Colonel," "Mr. and Mrs. Dove," "An Ideal Family," "Her First Ball," "The Voyage," "Marriage à la Mode," "At the Bay," "The Garden Party," "The Singing Lesson."

In a German Pension. London: Stephen Swift, 1911. "The Child-Who-Was-Tired," "Germans at Meat," "The Baron," "The Luft Bad," "At Lehmann's," "Frau Brechenmacher Attends a Wedding," "The Sister of the Baroness," "Frau Fischer," "A Birthday," "The Modern Soul," "The Advanced Lady," "The Swing of the Pendulum," "A Blaze."

Katherine Mansfield: The Woman and the Writer. Edited by Gillian Boddy. Ringwood, Australia: Penguin Books, 1988. "The Education of Audrey," "Frau Brechenmacher Attends a Wedding," "The Woman at the Store," "Old Tar," "The Wind Blows," "Bliss," "Pictures," "The Daughters of the Late Colonel," "At the Bay," "The Doll's House," "The Fly."

The Short Stories of Katherine Mansfield. Introduction by J. M. Murry. New York: Knopf, 1937.

Something Childish and Other Stories. London: Constable, 1924. Also entitled *The Little Girl and Other Stories.* New York: Knopf, 1924. "The Tiredness of Rosabel," "How Pearl Button Was Kidnapped," "The Journey to Bruges," "A Truthful Adventure," "New Dresses," "The Woman at the Store," "Ole Underwood," "The Little Girl," "Millie," "Pension Seguin," "Violet," "Bains Turcs," "Something Childish but Very Natural,"

"An Indiscreet Journey," "Spring Pictures," "Late at Night," "Two Tuppenny Ones, Please," "The Black Cap," "A Suburban Fairy Tale," "Carnation," "See-Saw," "This Flower," "The Wrong House," "Sixpence," "Poison."

Stories by Katherine Mansfield. Introduction by Elizabeth Bowen. New York: Vintage Books, 1956. "The Tiredness of Rosabel," "The Baron," "The Modern Soul," "The Woman at the Store," "Ole Underwood," "The Little Governess," "Prelude," "At the Bay," "Psychology," "Bliss," *Je ne parle pas français,* "Sun and Moon," "This Flower," "The Man without a Temperament," "Revelations," "The Young Girl," "The Stranger," "The Daughters of the Late Colonel," "Life of Ma Parker," "The Singing Lesson," "The Voyage," "The Garden Party," "Miss Brill," "Marriage à la Mode," "The Doll's House," "The Doves' Nest," "Six Years After."

Stories (or Novels) Published Separately

The Aloe (with Prelude). Edited by Vincent O'Sullivan. Wellington, New Zealand: Port Nicholson Press, 1982.
Je ne parle pas français. Hampstead, England: Heron Press, 1920.
Prelude. Richmond, England: Hogarth Press, 1918.

Poetry

Poems, ed. J. M. Murry. London: Constable, 1923. New York: Knopf, 1924.

Nonfiction

The Collected Letters of Katherine Mansfield. Vol. 1, 1903–17. Edited by Vincent O'Sullivan and Margaret Scott. Oxford: Oxford University Press, 1984.
The Collected Letters of Katherine Mansfield. Vol. 2, 1918–19. Edited by Vincent O'Sullivan and Margaret Scott. Oxford: Oxford University Press, 1987.
Journal of Katherine Mansfield. Edited by J. M. Murry. London: Constable, 1927; New York: Knopf, 1927.
Journal of Katherine Mansfield. "Definitive Edition." Edited by J. M. Murry. London: Constable, 1954.
Katherine Mansfield's Letters to John Middleton Murry, 1913–1922. Edited by J. M. Murry. London: Constable, 1951; New York: Knopf, 1951.
The Letters of Katherine Mansfield. Edited by J. M. Murry. 2 vols. London: Constable, 1928; New York: Knopf, 1929.
Novels and Novelists. Edited by J. M. Murry. Book reviews. London: Constable, 1930; New York: Knopf, 1930.
The Scrapbook of Katherine Mansfield. Edited by J. M. Murry. London: Constable, 1939; New York: Knopf, 1940.

Secondary Works

Interview

Orage, A. R. "Talks with Katherine Mansfield." In *Selected Essays and Critical Writings*, edited by Herbert Read and Denis Saurat. Reprint. Freeport, N.Y.: Books for Libraries Press, 1967.

Books

Alpers, Antony. *The Life of Katherine Mansfield*. New York: Viking Press, 1980.

Baker, Ida. *Katherine Mansfield: The Memories of LM*. London: Michael Joseph, 1971.

Beauchamp, Sir Harold. *Reminiscences and Recollections*. New Plymouth, New Zealand: T. Avery, 1937.

Berkman, Sylvia. *Katherine Mansfield: A Critical Study*. New Haven: Yale University Press, 1951.

Carswell, John. *Lives and Letters*. New Directions, 1978.

Cather, Willa. "Katherine Mansfield." In *Not under Forty*, 123–47. New York: Knopf, 1936.

Clarke, Isabel C. *Katherine Mansfield: A Biography*. Wellington: Beltane Book Bureau, 1944.

Daiches, David. *New Literary Values*. Edinburgh: Oliver & Boyd, 1936.

———. *The Novel and the Modern World*. Chicago: University of Chicago Press, 1939.

Daly, Saralyn R. *Katherine Mansfield*. New York: Twayne Publishers, 1965.

De La Bedoyere, Michael. "The Genius: Katherine Mansfield." In *An Infinity of Questions: A Study of the Religion of Art, and the Art of Religion in the Lives of Five Women*. London: Dennis Dobson, 1946.

Fullbrook, Kate. *Katherine Mansfield*. Bloomington: Indiana University Press, 1986.

Gordon, Ian A. *Katherine Mansfield*. London: Longmans, Green & Co., 1954.

Gurr, Andrew. *Writers in Exile: The Identity of Home in Modern Literature*. Atlantic Highlands, N.J.: Humanities Press, 1981.

Hankin, C. A. *Katherine Mansfield and Her Confessional Stories*. New York: St. Martin's Press, 1983.

Hanson, Clare, and Andrew Gurr. *Katherine Mansfield*. New York: St. Martin's Press, 1981.

Hormasji, Nariman. *Katherine Mansfield: An Appraisal*. London: Collins, 1967.

Lawrence, D. H. *The Letters of D. H. Lawrence*, edited by James T. Boulton. 4 vols. Cambridge: Cambridge University Press, 1981.

Lea, F. A. *The Life of John Middleton Murry*. New York: Oxford University Press, 1960.

Magalaner, Marvin. *The Fiction of Katherine Mansfield*. Carbondale: Southern Illinois University Press, 1971.

Meyers, Jeffrey. *Katherine Mansfield: A Biography*. New York: New Directions Press, 1978.

Murry, John Middleton. *The Problem of Style*. London: Oxford University Press, 1930.

———. *Between Two Worlds: An Autobiography*. London: Jonathan Cape, 1935.

———. *Katherine Mansfield and Other Literary Portraits*. London: Peter Nevill, 1949.

———. *Katherine Mansfield and Other Literary Studies*. London: Constable & Co., 1959.

———. *The Letters of John Middleton Murry to Katherine Mansfield*. Edited by C. A. Hankin. New York: Franklin Watts, 1983.

Orton, William. *The Last Romantic*. New York: Farrar & Rinehart, 1937.

Tomalin, Claire. *Katherine Mansfield: A Secret Life*. New York: Knopf, 1988.

Willy, Margaret. *Three Women Diarists: Celia Fiennes, Dorothy Wordsworth, Katherine Mansfield*. London: Longmans, Green & Co., 1964.

Articles

Alcock, Peter. "An Aloe in the Garden: Something Essentially New Zealand in Miss Mansfield." *Journal of Commonwealth Literature* 11(1977): 58–64.

Allbright, Rachel. "Katherine Mansfield and Wingley." *Folio* 24(1959): 23–29.

Armstrong, Martin. "The Art of Katherine Mansfield." *The Fortnightly Review* 113(1923): 484–90.

Assad, Thomas J. "Mansfield's 'The Fly.'" *Explicator* 14(1955): item 10.

Baldeshwiler, Eileen. "Katherine Mansfield's Theory of Fiction." *Studies in Short Fiction* 7(1970): 421–32.

Bateson, F. W., and B. Shahevitch. "Katherine Mansfield's 'The Fly.'" *Essays in Criticism* 12(1962): 39–53.

Beachcroft, T. O. "Katherine Mansfield's Encounter with Theocritus." *English* 115(1974): 113–19.

———. "Katherine Mansfield—Then and Now." *Modern Fiction Studies* 24(1978): 343–52.

Bell, Margaret. "In Memory of Katherine Mansfield." *American Bookman* 76(1933): 36–46.

Bell, Pauline P. "Mansfield's 'The Fly.'" *Explicator* 19(1960): item 20.

Blanchard, Lydia. "The Savage Pilgrimage of D. H. Lawrence and Katherine Mansfield: A Study in Literary Influence, Anxiety, and Subversion." *Modern Language Quarterly* 47(1986): 48–65.

Bledsoe, Thomas. "Mansfield's 'The Fly.'" *Explicator* 5(1945): item 53.

Boyle, Ted. "The Death of the Boss: Another Look at Katherine Mansfield's 'The Fly.'" *Modern Fiction Studies* 11(1965): 183–85.

Brett, Dorothy. "Katherine." *Adam International Review* 300(1966): 86–87.

Brophy, Brigid. "Katherine Mansfield's Self-Depiction." *Michigan Quarterly Review* 5(1966): 89–93.

Burgan, Mary. "Childbirth Trauma in Katherine Mansfield's Early Stories." *Modern Fiction Studies* 24(1978): 395–412.

Cazamian, Louis. "D. H. Lawrence and Katherine Mansfield as Letter Writers." *University of Toronto Quarterly*, 3(1934): 286–307.

Conroy, Geraldine L. "'Our Perhaps Uncommon Friendship': The Relationship between S. S. Koteliansky and Katherine Mansfield." *Modern Fiction Studies* 24(1978): 355–67.

Cox, Sidney. "The Fastidiousness of Katherine Mansfield." *Sewanee Review* 39(1931): 158–69.

Davis, Robert Murray. "The Unity of 'The Garden Party.'" *Studies in Short Fiction* 2(1964): 61–65.

Delany, Paul. "Short and Simple Annals of the Poor: Katherine Mansfield's 'The Doll's House.'" *Mosaic* 10(1976): 6–17.

Dinkins, Paul. "Katherine Mansfield: The Ending." *Southwest Review* 38(1953): 203–10.

Dowling, David. "Mansfield's 'Something Childish but Very Natural.'" *Explicator* 38(1980): 44–45.

Eisinger, Chester. "Mansfield's 'Bliss.'" *Explicator* 7(1949): item 48.

Franklin, Carol. "Mansfield and Richardson: A Short Story Dialectic." *Australian Literary Studies* 11(1983): 227–33.

Freeman, Kathleen. "The Art of Katherine Mansfield," *The Canadian Forum* 7(1927): 302–7.

Gargano, James. "Mansfield's 'Miss Brill.'" *Explicator* 19(1960): item 10.

Garlington, Jack. "Katherine Mansfield: The Critical Trend." *Twentieth-Century Literature* 2(1956): 51–61.

———. "An Unattributed Story by Katherine Mansfield?" *Modern Language Notes* 71(1956): 91–93.

Greenfield, Stanley. "Mansfield's 'The Fly.'" *Explicator* 17(1958): item 2.

Greenwood, E. B., and F. W. Bateson. "More on 'The Fly.'" *Essays in Criticism* 12(1962): 448–52.

Gubar, Susan. "The Birth of the Artist as Heroine: (Re)production, the *Kunstlerroman* Tradition, and the Fiction of Katherine Mansfield." In *The Representation of Women in Fiction*, 19–59, edited by Carolyn G. Heilbrun and Margaret R. Higonnet. Baltimore: Johns Hopkins University Press, 1983.

Hagopian, John T. "Capturing Mansfield's 'Fly.'" *Modern Fiction Studies* 9(1963): 385–90.

Hankin, Cherry. "Fantasy and the Sense of an Ending in the Work of Katherine Mansfield." *Modern Fiction Studies* 24(1978): 465–74.

Hubbell, George Shelton. "Katherine Mansfield and Kezia." *Sewanee Review* 25(1927): 325–35.

Hudson, Stephen (Sidney Schiff). "First Meetings with Katherine Mansfield." *Cornhill Magazine* 170(1958): 202–12.

Hull, Robert L. "Alienation in 'Miss Brill.'" *Studies in Short Fiction* 5(1967): 74–76.

Hynes, Sam. "Katherine Mansfield: The Defeat of the Personal." *South Atlantic Quarterly* 52(1953): 555–60.

Iverson, Anders. "A Reading of Katherine Mansfield's 'The Garden-Party.'" *Orbis Letterarum* 23(1968): 5–34.

Jacobs, Willis D. "Mansfield's 'The Fly.'" *Explicator* 5(1947): item 32.

Justus, James H. "Katherine Mansfield: The Triumph of Egoism." *Mosaic* 6(1973): 13–22.

Klein, Don W. "Katherine Mansfield and the Prisoner of Love." *Critique* 3(1960): 20–33.

———. "The Chekovian Source of 'Marriage à la Mode.'" *Philological Quarterly* 42(1963): 284–88.

———. "'The Garden-Party': A Portrait of the Artist." *Criticism* 5(1963): 360–71.

———. "An Eden for Insiders: Katherine Mansfield's New Zealand." *College English* 27(1965): 201–9.

———. "Mansfield and the Orphans of Time." *Modern Fiction Studies* 24(1978): 423–38.

Kobler, J. F. "The Sexless Narrator of Mansfield's 'The Young Girl.'" *Studies in Short Fiction* 17(1980): 269–74.

McLaughlin, Ann L. "The Same Job: The Shared Writing Aims of Katherine Mansfield and Virginia Woolf." *Modern Fiction Studies* 24(1978): 369–82.

Madden, David. "Katherine Mansfield's 'Miss Brill.'" *University Review* 31(1964): 89–92.

———. "Traces of Her 'Self' in Katherine Mansfield's 'Bliss.'" *Modern Fiction Studies* 24(1978): 413–22.

Michel-Michot, Paulette. "Katherine Mansfield's 'The Fly': An Attempt to Capture the Boss." *Studies in Short Fiction* 11(1974): 85–92.

Murry, Mary Middleton. "Katherine Mansfield and John Middleton Murry." *London Magazine* 6(1959): 69–71.

Neaman, Judith S. "Allusion, Image, and Associative Pattern: The Answers in Mansfield's 'Bliss.'" *Twentieth-Century Literature* 32(1986): 242–54.

Nebeker, Helen S. "The Pear Tree: Sexual Implications in Katherine Mansfield's 'Bliss.'" *Modern Fiction Studies* 18(1972): 545–51.

O'Connor, Frank. "Katherine Mansfield." In *The Lonely Voice: A Study of the Short Story*, 128–42. New York: World Publishing, 1962.

Oleson, Clinton W. "'The Fly' Rescued." *College English* 22(1961): 585.

Peterson, Richard F. "The Circle of Truth: The Stories of Katherine Mansfield and Mary Lavin." *Modern Fiction Studies* 24(1978): 383–94.

Porter, Katherine Anne. "The Art of Katherine Mansfield." *Nation* 145(1937): 435–36.

Rankin, William. "Ineffability in the Fiction of Jean Toomer and Katherine Mansfield." In *Renaissance and Modern: Essays in Honor of Edwin M. Moseley*, 160–71. Syracuse, N.Y.: Syracuse University Press, 1976.

Rea, J. "Mansfield's 'The Fly.'" *Explicator* 23(1965): item 68.

Robinson, Fred. C. "Mansfield's 'The Garden-Party.'" *Explicator* 24(1966): item 66.

Schneider, Elisabeth. "Katherine Mansfield and Chekhov." *Modern Language Notes* 50(1935): 394–97.

Sorkin, Adam J. "Katherine Mansfield's 'The Garden-Party': Style and Social Occasion." *Modern Fiction Studies* 24(1978): 439–55.

Stallman, Robert Wooster. "Mansfield's 'The Fly.'" *Explicator* 3(1945): item 49.

Stanley, C. W. "The Art of Katherine Mansfield." *Dalhousie Review* 10(1930): 26–41.

Sutherland, Ronald. "Katherine Mansfield: Plagiarist, Disciple, or Ardent Admirer?" *Critique* 5(1962): 58–75.

Taylor, Donald S., and Daniel A. Weiss. "Crashing the 'Garden-Party.'" *Modern Fiction Studies* 4(1958): 361–64.

Thomas, J. D. "The Anatomy of a Fly." *College English* 22(1961): 586.

———. "Symbol and Parallelism in 'The Fly.'" *College English* 22(1961): 256, 261–62.

Van Kranendonk, A. G. "Katherine Mansfield." *English Studies* 12(1930): 49–57.

Wagenknecht, Edward. "Katherine Mansfield." *The English Journal* 17(1928): 272–84.

———. "Dickens and Katherine Mansfield." *Dickensian* 26(1929): 15–23.

Waldron, Philip. "Katherine Mansfield's *Journal*." *Twentieth-Century Literature* 20(1974): 11–18.

Walker, Warren. "The Unresolved Conflict in 'The Garden-Party.'" *Modern Fiction Studies* 3(1957): 354–58.

Whitridge, Arnold. "Katherine Mansfield." *Sewanee Review* 48(1940): 256–72.

Wright, Celeste Turner. "Darkness as a Symbol in Katherine Mansfield." *Modern Philology* 51(1954): 204–7.

———. "Mansfield's 'The Fly.'" *Explicator* 12(1954): item 27.

———. "Genesis of a Short Story." *Philological Quarterly* 34(1955): 91–96.

———. "Katherine Mansfield's Boat Image." *Twentieth-Century Literature* 1(1955): 128–32.

―――. "Katherine Mansfield's Dog Image." *Literature and Psychology* 10(1960): 80–81.

Zinman, Toby Silverman. "The Snail under the Leaf: Katherine Mansfield's Imagery." *Modern Fiction Studies* 24(1978): 457–64.

Zorn, Marilyn. "Visionary Flowers: Another Study of Katherine Mansfield's 'Bliss.'" *Studies in Short Fiction* 17(1980): 141–47.

Bibliographies

Bardas, Mary Louise. "The State of Scholarship on Katherine Mansfield, 1950-1970." *World Literature Written in English* 11(1972): 77–93.

Humanities Research Center. *Katherine Mansfield: An Exhibition.* Catalog of the holdings in the REEM Collection. Austin: University of Texas, 1973.

Meyers, Jeffrey. "Katherine Mansfield: A Bibliography of International Criticism, 1921–1977." *Bulletin of Bibliography* 34(1977): 53–67.

―――. "Katherine Mansfield: A Selected Checklist." *Modern Fiction Studies* 24(1978): 475–76.

Morris, G. N. Introduction to *Mansfieldiana: A Brief Katherine Mansfield Bibliography.* Wellington: Beltane Book Bureau, 1948.

Index

The Author

J. F. Kobler is a professor of English at the University of North Texas. He obtained his Ph.D. from the University of Texas. His publications on the works of Ernest Hemingway, William Faulkner, Randall Jarrell, and Katherine Mansfield consist of numerous articles and one book, *Ernest Hemingway: Journalist and Artist*. He has served as president of the College English Association and the South Central Modern Language Association and has done stints as director of freshman composition and of graduate studies at UNT. Prior to entering the academic world, he was a reporter for newspapers in Shreveport, Louisiana, and Houston and for United Press in New Orleans.

The Editor

Gordon Weaver earned his Ph.D. in English and creative writing at the University of Denver in 1970, and is currently professor of English at Oklahoma State University. He is the author of several novels, including *Count a Lonely Cadence, Give Him a Stone, Circling Byzantium,* and most recently *The Eight Corners of the World.* His short stories are collected in *The Entombed Man of Thule, Such Waltzing Was Not Easy, Getting Serious, Morality Play,* and *A World Quite Round.* Recognition of his fiction includes the St. Lawrence Award for Fiction (1973), two National Endowment for the Arts fellowships (1974 and 1989), and the O. Henry First Prize (1979). He edited *The American Short Story, 1945–1980: A Critical History* and is currently editor of the *Cimarron Review.* Married and the father of three daughters, he lives in Stillwater, Oklahoma.